'Some Friends Came to See Us': Lord Moyne's 1936 Expedition to the Asmat

Nick Stanley

The British Museum

Published with the generous support of
Furthermore: a program of the J. M. Kaplan Fund

Furthermore:
a program of the J.M. Kaplan Fund

Publishers
The British Museum
Great Russell Street
London WC1B 3DG

Series editor
Sarah Faulks

'Some Friends Came to See Us':
Lord Moyne's 1936 Expedition to the Asmat
Nick Stanley

ISBN 978 086159 206 7
ISSN 1747 3640

Front cover: Asmat men in canoes on the Eilanden River, 1936. Photograph taken by A. Pereira. RAI 7193

Printed and bound in the UK by 4edge Ltd, Hockley

Papers used by The British Museum are recyclable products made from wood grown in well-managed forests and other controlled sources. The manufacturing processes conform to the environmental regulations of the country of origin.

Further information about the Museum and its collection can be found at britishmuseum.org.

Contents

Acknowledgements	iv
Image Sources and Abbreviations	v
Map	vi
Introduction	1
1. Setting the Scene	5
2. Making Contact	17
3. Gifts and Exchanges on the Eilanden and Kampong Rivers	31
4. Creating the Record	39
5. Conclusions	48
References	52
Index	54

Acknowledgements

I would like to express my sincere thanks to Dr Lissant Bolton, Keeper of the Department of Africa, Oceania and the Americas at the British Museum, who has given me a most congenial academic and sociable home for the past six years. Her support and enthusiasm for my work in West Papua has been crucial for all I have written during this time and for the current publication. I am also grateful to all members of the department, especially Jim Hamill and Jill Hasell for their assistance with archival and artefact research.

My second debt is to those who have so kindly provided me with the photographs reproduced here. The oldest images from the early 20th century have been supplied by the Nationaal Museum van Wereldculturen, Amsterdam. The Guinness family have shared Lord Moyne's early photographs, which have not been reproduced before, and the Delves Broughton family have given me access to Lady Vera Delves Broughton's albums of 1935 and 1936. Lord Arthur Elveden's family have made available the original reels of his film of the Walkabout expedition of 1936. I would like to thank the British Museum and the Royal Anthropological Institute for their permission to reproduce photographs deeded to them by Lord Moyne and Lady Vera Delves Broughton. I am very grateful to Sarah Walpole, Archive Officer at the RAI, for making available copies of the photographs from the extensive Delves Broughton archive. I have also had the great good fortune to share with the Film Officer of the RAI, Susanne Hammacher, the excitement of the restoration of the Walkabout film material. The search for this material was inspired by Professor Nicholas Thomas, but without Susanne Hammacher's work the digital film copies would not have been made. The restoration of this film by Joao de Oliveira of Prestech Ltd has been funded by the generous support of both Guinness and Delves Broughton family members, the Barness Trust, the Department of Africa, Oceania and the Americas at the British Museum, Diageo plc and The Walter Edward Guinness Educational Trust. I am very pleased that it has been possible to use stills from this material in the current volume.

I would also like to thank those who have helped in the production of this monograph. Anthony Leigh has rephotographed and enhanced the quality of key images used from the Moyne 1929 album and the 1936 Delves Broughton album. Susanne Hammacher has provided the film stills reproduced here. Thanks are also due to those who have reviewed this text: Dr Lissant Bolton, Dr Ben Burt, Dr Sean Kingston, Professor Darren Newbury, Sarah Walpole, and the academic reviewers, Dr Karen Jacobs and Dr Michael Scott, and also my editor, Sarah Faulks, at the British Museum. Finally I would like to thank Furthermore: a program of the J. M. Kaplan Fund for a publication grant towards the cost of this book. I am, of course, solely responsible for any mistakes that remain in this work.

Image Sources and Abbreviations

BM Oc,B28 series: photographic prints deposited at the British Museum by Lord Moyne.

BM Oc1934,0316 series and **BM Oc1936,0720** series: catalogue entries of artefacts deposited by Lord Moyne in 1934 and 1936 at the British Museum.

'Eastern Cruise 1934/35' album: photographs taken by Lady Vera Delves Broughton and held by the Delves Broughton family.

'Eastern Trip 1935–36' album: photographs taken by Lady Vera Delves Broughton in 1936 and given to Lord Arthur Elveden, held by the Elveden family.

RAI 400 series: photographs deposited at the Royal Anthropological Institute by Lord Moyne in 1936 and taken by Lady Delves Broughton and Arthur Pereira in 1936 with some prints from 1935 interspersed.

TM series: images from *Nova Guinea* (1923) held by Nationaal Museum van Wereldculturen, Tropenmuseum, Amsterdam.

'Transfer film footage': from Asmat New Guinea, Rennell and Bellona, Solomon Islands, 1936, taken by Lady Delves Broughton and held in RAI film archives.

'Travels WEG' album: photographs taken by Lord Moyne in 1929 and held by the Guinness family.

Walkabout film: Walkabout film taken by Viscount Elveden during the 1936 Walkabout trip, restored in 2016 and held in the RAI film archive.

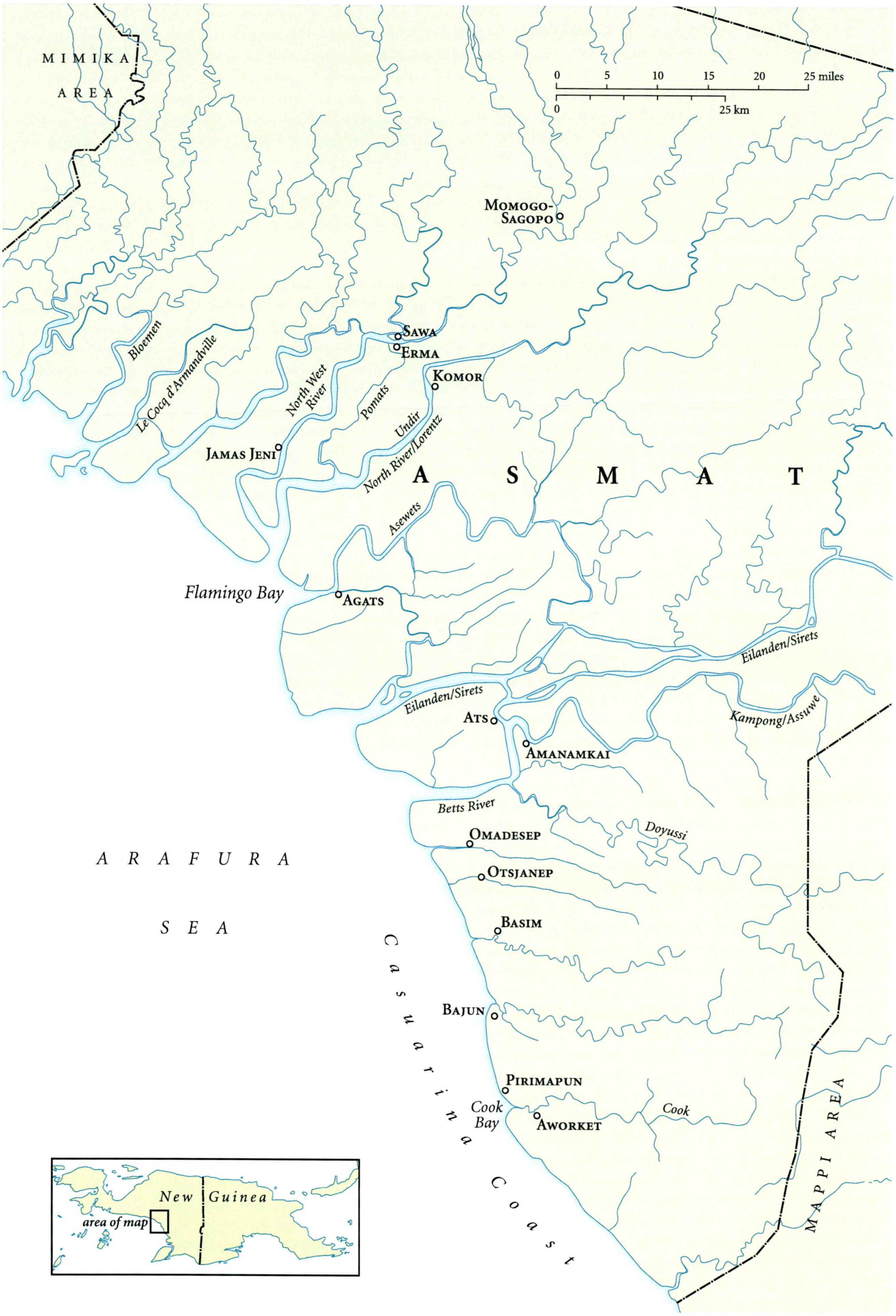

Figure 1 Map of Asmat area, showing the key sites and rivers mentioned in the text (map by Martin Brown)

Introduction

This publication seeks to bring together a range of written and visual sources to create a narrative of a unique encounter that has both historical and contemporary importance. Prior to Moyne's expeditions, there had been only fleeting recorded interactions between the Asmat people of South New Guinea and European explorers (Bloemen 1998; see **Figs 7–8**). Moyne's three visits to the region are notable in that they occurred over a seven-year period. The publication brings together the key sources documenting this first significant interaction, highlighting in particular Moyne's last visit to Asmat in 1936. At the same time, this study serves as an important archive of a key period in the Asmat past. Subsequent major social and political changes since the historic meetings have meant that many aspects of the Asmat way of life have consequently been largely forgotten or ignored.

The title of this work is taken from Lord Moyne's account of his adventures in Papua. His use of the term 'friends' to describe the Asmat, a group of people widely feared throughout the region, is interesting. Was the word being used ironically? I suggest not; rather, Moyne was making an implicit but nevertheless strong claim to have achieved friendly relationships despite the mutual suspicion in which initially both parties held each other. What Moyne was also celebrating was his ability to generate a real engagement with this people in a way that had hardly been accomplished before. Rather than irony, there is in this account, both written and photographic, a genuine affection for the people he met on three different occasions.

This work focuses on the important documentation of Asmat society in the photographs, collections and recollections that Moyne's expeditions produced. The voyages were also a kind of adventure probably only possible at this point in the 20th century. This introduction provides the context for Moyne's adventure. Chapter 1 explores the friendly relationship Moyne established with the Asmat in contrast to other previous encounters with Asmat people. Chapter 2 chronicles the sequence of visits to the major waterways on which the Asmat lived, while Chapter 3 gives an account of the gift exchanges that took place. Chapter 4 documents the making of an ethnographic collection, its subsequent exhibition in Britain and its importance today for contemporary craft production in Asmat. The conclusion reviews the significance of both these photographs and artefacts today in sustaining a vibrant Asmat aesthetic and economy.

Why, on all three voyages, did Moyne seek out the Asmat region? There was a strong flavour of pure adventure in his thinking. He wrote: 'Although we had to make certain preparations in advance, we kept our plans as fluid as possible' (Moyne 1936a: 9), explaining that he sought 'to find regions which have baffled penetration by aeroplane and motor car' (Moyne 1936a: 2). The expedition provided a more publicly responsible objective too, making 'a collection of ethnographical material for the British Museum and London Zoo' (Moyne 1936a: 1). He chose a place where there was no colonial infrastructure and where he would have unmediated contact with people living self-sufficient lives and with little contact with the outside world. As he explained: 'My own instinct has always been to get away from the great ports and centres of modern life and to visit human races, birds and beasts, rivers, mountains and forests where they

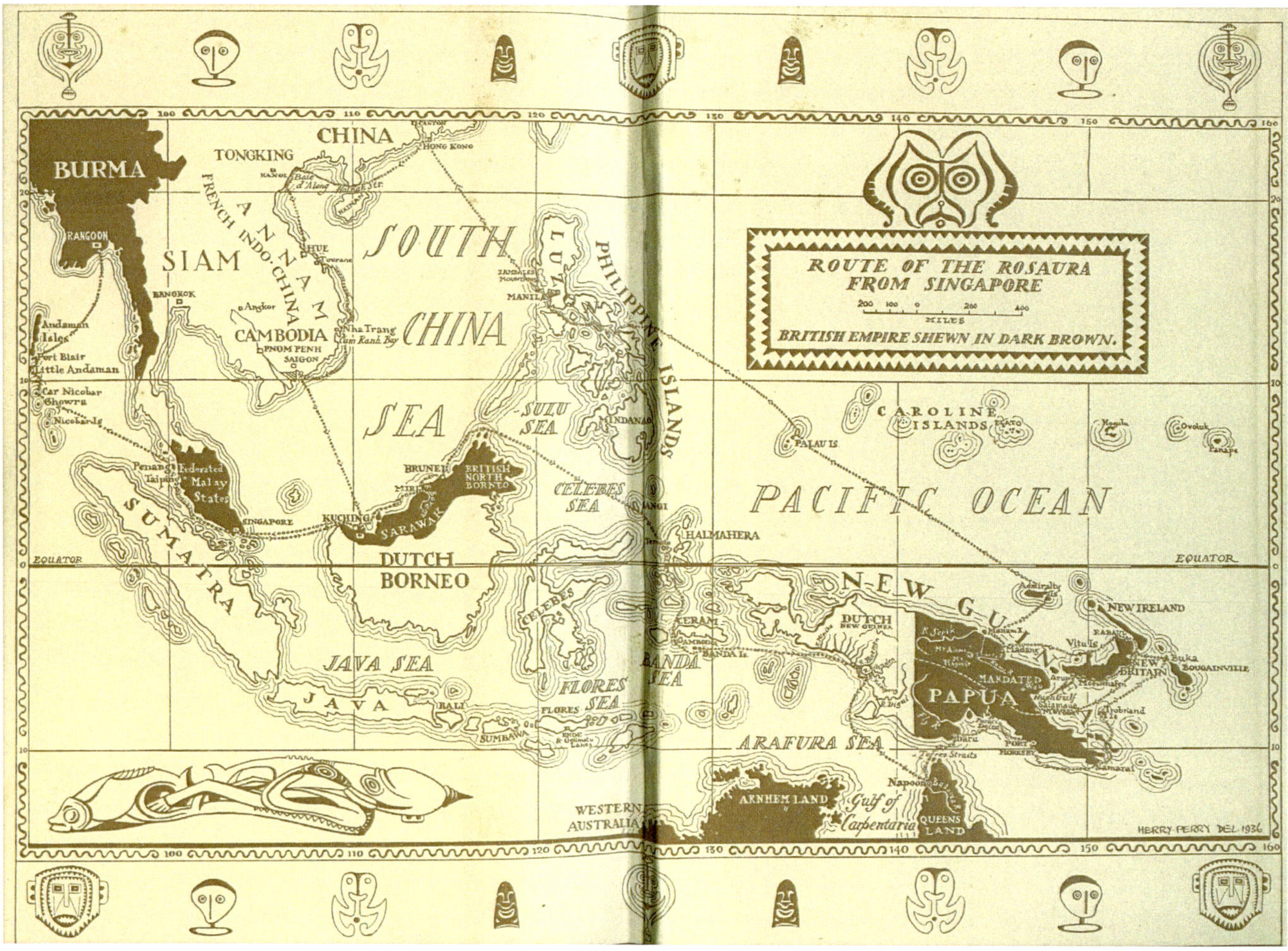

Figure 2 Map showing the itinerary for Lord Moyne's 1935/6 'Eastern Trip' printed on the inside front cover of *Walkabout* (Moyne 1936a)

Figure 3 Pages of photographs taken in Papua by Lord Moyne in 1929 reproduced in 'WEG 1929'album

still remain untouched by Western development' (Moyne 1936a: 1). South Papua fitted such specifications admirably.

The Asmat region consists of an area of 27,000 square kilometres of river deltas which form a vast alluvial swamp with tides that stretch many kilometres upstream. To the north is a brief stretch of savannah beneath the Jayawijaya Mountains. These mountains, which rise to a height of 4884 metres, are some of the steepest and tallest on the equator, even boasting glaciers. The Jayawijaya range forms the northern border and barrier whilst to the south the Arafura Sea, shallow and treacherous, is similarly inhospitable. What distinguishes the northern and central part of the area is the lack of fixed topographic features. There is no stone or other solid material apart from vegetation such as grass or wood. This is a land consisting almost entirely of mud. The rivers shift their courses continuously and water penetrates into every nook and cranny. The result is a seemingly featureless landscape of riverbanks and dense spongy jungle only recognisable to those who know the territory intimately through daily travel. The annual rainfall is 200 inches

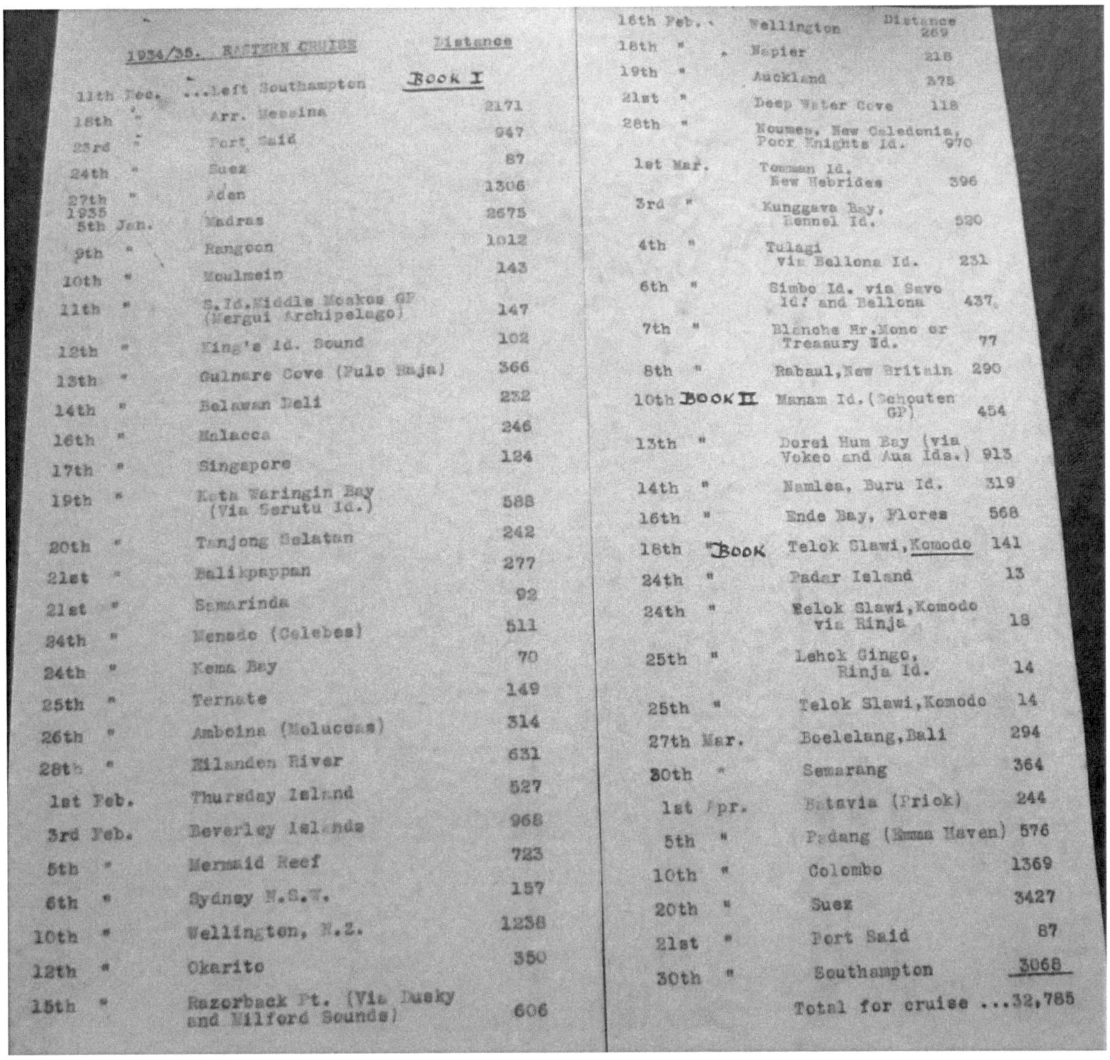

1934/35. EASTERN CRUISE		Distance
11th Dec.	...Left Southampton BOOK I	
18th "	Arr. Messina	2171
23rd "	Port Said	947
24th "	Suez	87
27th "	Aden	1306
1935 5th Jan.	Madras	2675
9th "	Rangoon	1012
10th "	Moulmein	143
11th "	S. Id. Middle Moskos GP (Mergui Archipelago)	147
12th "	King's Id. Sound	102
13th "	Gulnare Cove (Pulo Baja)	366
14th "	Belawan Deli	232
16th "	Malacca	246
17th "	Singapore	124
19th "	Kota Waringin Bay (Via Serutu Id.)	588
20th "	Tanjong Selatan	242
21st "	Balikpapan	277
21st "	Samarinda	92
24th "	Menado (Celebes)	511
24th "	Kema Bay	70
25th "	Ternate	149
26th "	Amboina (Moluccas)	314
28th "	Eilanden River	631
1st Feb.	Thursday Island	527
3rd Feb.	Beverley Islands	968
5th "	Mermaid Reef	723
6th "	Sydney N.S.W.	157
10th "	Wellington, N.Z.	1258
12th "	Okarito	350
15th "	Razorback Pt. (Via Dusky and Milford Sounds)	606
16th Feb.	Wellington	269
18th "	Napier	218
19th "	Auckland	375
21st "	Deep Water Cove	118
28th "	Noumea, New Caledonia, Poor Knights Id.	970
1st Mar.	Tomman Id. New Hebrides	396
3rd "	Kunggava Bay, Rennel Id.	520
4th "	Tulagi via Bellona Id.	231
6th "	Simbo Id. via Savo Id. and Bellona	437
7th "	Blanche Hr. Mono or Treasury Id.	77
8th "	Rabaul, New Britain	290
10th BOOK II	Manam Id. (Schouten GP)	454
13th "	Dorei Hum Bay (via Yokeo and Aua Ids.)	913
14th "	Namlea, Buru Id.	319
16th "	Ende Bay, Flores	568
18th " BOOK	Telok Slawi, Komodo	141
24th "	Padar Island	13
24th "	Telok Slawi, Komodo via Rinja	18
25th "	Lehok Singo, Rinja Id.	14
25th "	Telok Slawi, Komodo	14
27th Mar.	Boelelang, Bali	294
30th "	Semarang	364
1st Apr.	Batavia (Priok)	244
5th "	Padang (Emma Haven)	576
10th "	Colombo	1369
20th "	Suez	3427
21st "	Port Said	87
30th "	Southampton	3068
	Total for cruise ...	32,785

Figure 4 Itinerary for Moyne's second voyage in 1934–5 printed in the inside front cover of Lady Delves Broughton's 'Eastern Cruise 1934/35' album

(500cm) and the temperature ranges from 27 to 33 degrees. It is no coincidence that the Dutch chose Tanah Merah on the Digul River to the east of Asmat in South Papua to build a jail to 'intern and often inter' the most prominent members of the anti-colonial revolt in Java in 1926 (Anderson 1991: 176). This was almost *terra incognita*, an impenetrable jungle swamp. Today, the jungle remains, but the villages are now built on piles at the riverbank with raised walkways and many houses have diesel-generated electricity. However, the topography of the region still makes travel arduous even by motorboat. The same problems of unseen obstacles such as logs hidden beneath the surface of the rivers makes navigation perilous and there are as yet no roads.

In the map illustrated here (**Fig. 1**), the location of the Asmat region within the island of New Guinea is shown in the bottom left-hand corner. The river system is depicted, with the Bloemen River appearing at the top left. In the centre of the map the Eilanden River stretches from the Arafura Sea to the foothills of Jayawijaya Mountains in the east. The Kampong River branches off and runs roughly parallel to the Eilanden before turning south into the Mappi region. The Doyussi River is the most southerly branch of the Eilanden River. All of these rivers feature in this story.

Moyne's trip to Asmat in 1936 was extensively documented and showed in considerable detail the interaction between locals and visitors. The record of this meeting is important on at least two counts. It provides access to contexts from which objects now in major collections, such as that of the British Museum, have come, and it preserves the complex picture of an otherwise rarely documented people. The documentation of this and the previous two visits by Moyne to Asmat is currently dispersed quite widely and this is the first attempt to bring the material together. The principal written source is *Walkabout: A Journey in Lands between the Pacific and Indian Oceans* (referred to in this book as *Walkabout*), and as the title indicates, Lord Moyne's account of his third visit to Asmat was part of the tale of the larger six months' voyage (November 1935 to April 1936) that took place in Borneo, Northern Australia, the Mandated Territory of New Guinea, the Philippines, China, Cambodia, the Federated Malay States, the Andaman and Nicobar Islands and Burma (**Fig. 2**).

He had an early trip in 1929 when he spent two weeks in Asmat (**Fig. 3**). A second voyage was of four months' duration (11 November 1934 to 30 April 1935), with his stay in Asmat lasting just under a week. Delves Broughton's album traces the itinerary of this trip (**Fig. 4**).

Moyne's account of his third voyage was published in September 1936, five months after his return to England. *Walkabout* (Moyne 1936a) contains 97 photographs, 13 of which relate to Asmat and all taken by Lady Vera Delves Broughton. She and Lord Moyne gave copies of these and other photographs to the British Museum, The Pitt Rivers Museum, the Royal Anthropological Institute (RAI) and another set of similar photographs made by a professional photographer on the trip, Arthur Pereira, to Cambridge University Museum of Archaeology and Ethnology (renamed the Museum of Archaeology and Anthropology in 1978). Both the Guinness and Delves Broughton families have albums relating to all three of the visits. Lady Delves Broughton also left a small suitcase at the RAI which has both prints and negatives of her work and three reels of film stock taken in 1936. Lord Elveden, Lord Moyne's nephew, also shot seven reels of film taken on the voyage in 1936. Recently it has been possible to recover the damaged film stock and recreate the film in its entirety, and copies of the restored film are now lodged in the RAI film archives. The film, referred to in this book as 'The Walkabout film', closely follows the narrative of Lord Moyne's text. The Walkabout project as a whole is, then, a well-resourced visual account, and the portion relating to Asmat is particularly richly documented. The intention of this publication is to bring together written accounts, a range of photographs, 16mm film material, objects collected during the voyages, most of which are now in museums, and details of the subsequent display of objects and photographs in a public exhibition in London in 1936. Together all of these sources can be seen as contributing to a single 'Walkabout archive', documenting an otherwise unrecorded period of a pre-colonial Papuan people.

This story has a particular connection to the British Museum. Moyne looked to the Museum, and in particular to H.J. Braunholtz, the Keeper of Ethnography, for advice when planning his excursions and he was especially keen to fill 'gaps' in the Museum's Melanesian collections. Moyne commented: 'I found that the art of this Dutch region was entirely unrepresented in the British Museum. I therefore wished to collect further examples of native handicraft from here' (Moyne 1936a: 3). Braunholtz was also involved in the Royal Anthropological Institute and introduced Moyne there as well at other museums in Britain. Moyne, in turn, donated collections of artefacts to the British Museum, 88 items in 1934 and 106 in 1936, as well as sets of photographs taken by Lady Delves Broughton and Arthur Pereira. Many of the photographs from the Walkabout tour are now publicly available on the British Museum website, and they are used in this publication as an aid to understanding the nature of the encounter.

Chapter 1
Setting the Scene

Friends?

In his account of his adventures in Papua and elsewhere in the Western Pacific, Lord Moyne wrote of his visit to the Eilanden River on the south coast of Papua in Netherlands New Guinea in February 1936: 'Some friends we made on a previous visit came out to see us in their big canoes (Plates 17 and 18).' Plate 17 (**Fig. 5**) in Moyne's *Walkabout* was captioned 'War-Canoe, Eilanden River' and Plate 18 (**Fig. 6**) 'Man with bone ornament through nasal septum offering to trade his shield, Eilanden River'.

These two iconic images raise a number of important questions about the provenance, construction and interpretation of the photographs. Of all the hundreds of images, taken during a few days in early 1936, these are perhaps the most intriguing in their possibilities and the issues that they raise: the first offering a placid distant view of rowers on the river whilst the second shows a close-up of direct engagement – angular, dynamic and intruding into the viewer's space.

In what sense could these visitors be 'friends'? And if they were friends, how had such a friendship blossomed in the most unpropitious of circumstances? As long as explorers or traders had arrived in the land of the Asmat there had been trouble. Early European navigators (Don Diego de Prado in 1607; Jan Carstensz in 1626; James Cook in 1770; John McCluerin 1792) were startled by the local people's display of hostility to the invasion of their privacy, and all employed guns to deter local men from attack (Bloemen 1998). The early encounters were 'fleeting, spasmodic, and given that they occurred generations apart, almost irrelevant' (Moore 2003: 75). The nature of these meetings meant that Papuans of the south coast would not enter the historic record as equal partners. Rather, the various explorers' accounts confirmed the same unchanging image of Papuans as always hostile and violent: 'wildness, savagery and bestiality were the dominant themes in most European imagery of Papuans during this

Figure 5 'War-Canoe, Eilanden River', 1936, reproduced as Plate 17 in *Walkabout* (Moyne 1936a). Photograph taken by Lady Delves Broughton. RAI 400.37734

Figure 6 'Man with bone ornament through nasal septum offering to trade his shield, Eilanden River', 1936, reproduced as Plate 18 in *Walkabout* (Moyne 1936a). Photograph taken by Lady Delves Broughton. British Museum, Oc,B94.11

Figure 7 'Boats from the Lorentz River', *Nova Guinea* VII 1923. Photograph taken by A. Pulle in 1909. TM- 10009503

early period' (Ballard 2001: 7). As Stasch has argued, there are two types of human condition posited in such a schema: 'the primitive as archaicness and stasis and the civilised as up-to-dateness and ceaseless innovation. Primitives live as they always have and thus represent the original state of humanity' (Stasch 2011: 6).

Perhaps the most celebrated such 'hostile and violent' encounter was recorded by James Cook in his account of his landing on 3 September 1770 at what was later to be called Cook Bay, near the site of the present village of Pirimapun on the Casuarina Coast. Cook was fairly reluctant to make a landing in the area, as 'it is only spending time to little purpose and carrying us far out of our way staying upon this coast, which is so shallow that we can hardly keep within sight of land'. As soon as his small party had landed from the tender he saw human footprints and set out for a walk along the shore. He and his party were attacked at once 'by three or four men who came out of the woods a little before us, but upon our immidiatly fireing (*sic*) upon them they retired' (Beaglehole 1955: 408). The Asmat were to be untroubled for well over a century after Cook's fleeting visit. The major ruler of Eastern Indonesia in the late 18th century, the Sultan of Tidore, did not venture into the area to enslave the Asmat as he did elsewhere in Papua. This suggests that the risks were too high to make the venture worthwhile. The same was true of the European blackbirders (recruiters of forced labour) who were kidnapping people elsewhere in the western Pacific in the 19th century. Similarly, during the hunt for birds of paradise feathers in the 19th and early 20th century to adorn fashion accessories in the West, hunters did not enter Asmat. As Swadling has observed: 'The intervening area, from the Otakwa River to the mouth of the Digul was avoided by plume hunters because of the known hostility of the Asmat towards foreigners' (Swadling 1996: 201). Later explorers such as Cecil Godfrey Rawlings marked their respect for and fear of all the south-coast people by describing them as 'hostile and treacherous inhabitants' (Rawlings 1913: 24). The effective quarantine of Asmat was based on the widespread perception of 'the aggressive hostility of its inhabitants who were feared as cannibals and head-hunters' (Helfrich 1996: 35). Their principal contact with their neighbours was through warfare in the pursuit of skulls. The Asmat people had little need to trade for practical resources as they had a plentiful supply of food in the form of sago and fish from the rivers.

West Papua was taken into Dutch colonial possession by proclamation in 1828. But the territory remained unexplored until the beginning of the 20th century and there was no knowledge of what resources the area contained. The first military expeditions by the Royal Netherlands Indies Army to the south coast (1904 and 1907) were confronted by Asmat warriors who objected to the presence of the colonial navy. As one account from the 1904 expedition explained:

> the two expedition ships were surrounded by native proas filled with standing, naked rowers who, following some peaceful exchanges of valuables soon became rowdy, obtrusive, theft-prone and aggressive. On one occasion the crew tried to cast the pushy Papuans off from their ship because they feared they were trying to board. Some blood was spilled, which so enraged the Papuans that they decided to put on a show of force. No fewer than 120 proas containing a total of some one thousand men surrounded the two ships.
> (van Duuren and Vink 2011: 61)

These 'proas' were single-hulled canoes. The expedition leaders, J.P. Meyjes and E.J. de Rochemont, decided to retreat in the face of such potential conflict. This account hints at the surprise and consternation that the Dutch felt at being bested by determined warriors who, without access to modern weaponry, nevertheless thwarted the military party's wish to explore and chart the river system.

The second expedition in 1909 sought to conquer Mount Wilhemina (Jayawijaya Mountain), but on their return from the mountains they also encountered the Asmat on the river (**Figs 7–8**). As Hendrikus Lorentz, the expedition leader reported: 'occasionally we received visits from Papuans alongside the ship. They made such a deafening noise that it was impossible to do anything. They remained wary and it was not possible to get them on board' (van Duuren and Vink 2011: 69).

Figure 8 'The expedition ship *Arend* on the Lorentz river encircled by Papua canoes from the south coast area', *Nova Guinea* VII 1923. Photograph taken by A. Pulle in 1909. TM-10009259

It was into this territory not yet subject to the colonial regime that Moyne chose to venture 20 years later, and like his European predecessors he faced potential danger. He recorded that his introduction to the area came from a New Zealand trader named Richard Roche whom he had first heard about through 'casual information obtained in the Dutch East Indies' in 1929 and who was described by Moyne as 'a wanderer from New Zealand' (Moyne 1936a: 3). Roche was based in Merauke, the only Dutch military post on the south coast of Papua. It had been set up in response to British complaints about head hunters raiding villages across the border into British New Guinea. Since 1924 Roche had spent months in the Asmat area, establishing trading relations and then buying birds of paradise feathers. Moyne stated that on his first visit Roche and his two companions were pursued by canoes up the Eilanden River: 'His Malay crew lost their nerve and turned back towards the sea. Encouraged by this evidence of fear the natives closed in on him and Roche was only able to escape by shooting the man in the front of each of the two leading canoes' (Moyne 1936a: 42). After establishing contact in 1929, Roche took Moyne 'by yacht and launch over two hundred miles of waterways on the Eilanden, Vriendschaps, Wildeman, Kampong and Doyussi rivers' (Moyne 1936a: 3) (see **Fig. 1**). This was an extensive tour that provided Moyne with a good introduction to the area. It also enabled him to establish relations with two villages on the Eilanden River, where he was able to collect 93 objects including paddles, spears, arrows and ten splendid shields (British Museum 1934; Moyne 1934). He also took a set of photographs of canoes and their rowers on the Eilanden River. When he decided to return for two further visits in 1935 and 1936 he lamented that Roche was no longer available to accompany him. The reason was simple. Moyne wrote: 'He [Roche] and his two pioneering friends have all three met violent and tragic deaths at the hands of the natives or lost in the forests of New Guinea' (Moyne 1936a: 21).

The Eilanden River, whose inhabitants Moyne described as ferocious, was the setting for the exchange captured in **Figure 6**. The friends' casual visit seems very puzzling in light of most previous encounters recorded between Asmat warriors and strangers. How could such a peaceful transaction have occurred? I think that the photographic record, together with Moyne's brief account of the event, helps explain this reception that was quite unlike anything that any previous visitor had experienced. However, some background factors need to be considered before seeking to explain Moyne's successful engagement with the local people, such as the biographical details of the visitors and their modes of travel. The response of their Asmat hosts is also vitally important, and in the absence of any written account the photographs help us gauge their reactions to the visitors.

The explorers

Lord Moyne (Walter Edward Guinness, 1880–1944, created first Lord Moyne in 1932) was full of both curiosity and adventurousness (Brodie 2008; Miley 2008) (**Fig. 9**). He was the third son of Cecil Guinness, head of the brewing company. In his youth he rowed for three years at Eton, where he became Captain of Boats, and as president of the Eton Society he was involved in expanding its remit to include academic debate. He was keenly interested in biology and considered studying the subject at Oxford but instead volunteered to fight in the Second Boer War in 1900. His other early adventures included a trip to China and Russia in 1902 that he wrote up in an account for his mother (Moyne 1950) and which was illustrated with his own architectural sketches. He also began game-hunting expeditions in the same year, although he later regretted hunting for purposes other than food. He entered parliament in 1907 and in the First World War he fought in Gallipoli and Egypt. He was a member of the Conservative government in 1922 as Under-Secretary for War, becoming First Secretary to the Treasury under the chancellorship of Winston Churchill in 1923. He was sworn in as a Privy Councillor in 1924 and became a cabinet minister for agriculture and fisheries from 1925 until the defeat of the Conservative government in 1929. At this point he decided to retire from politics, although he filled a

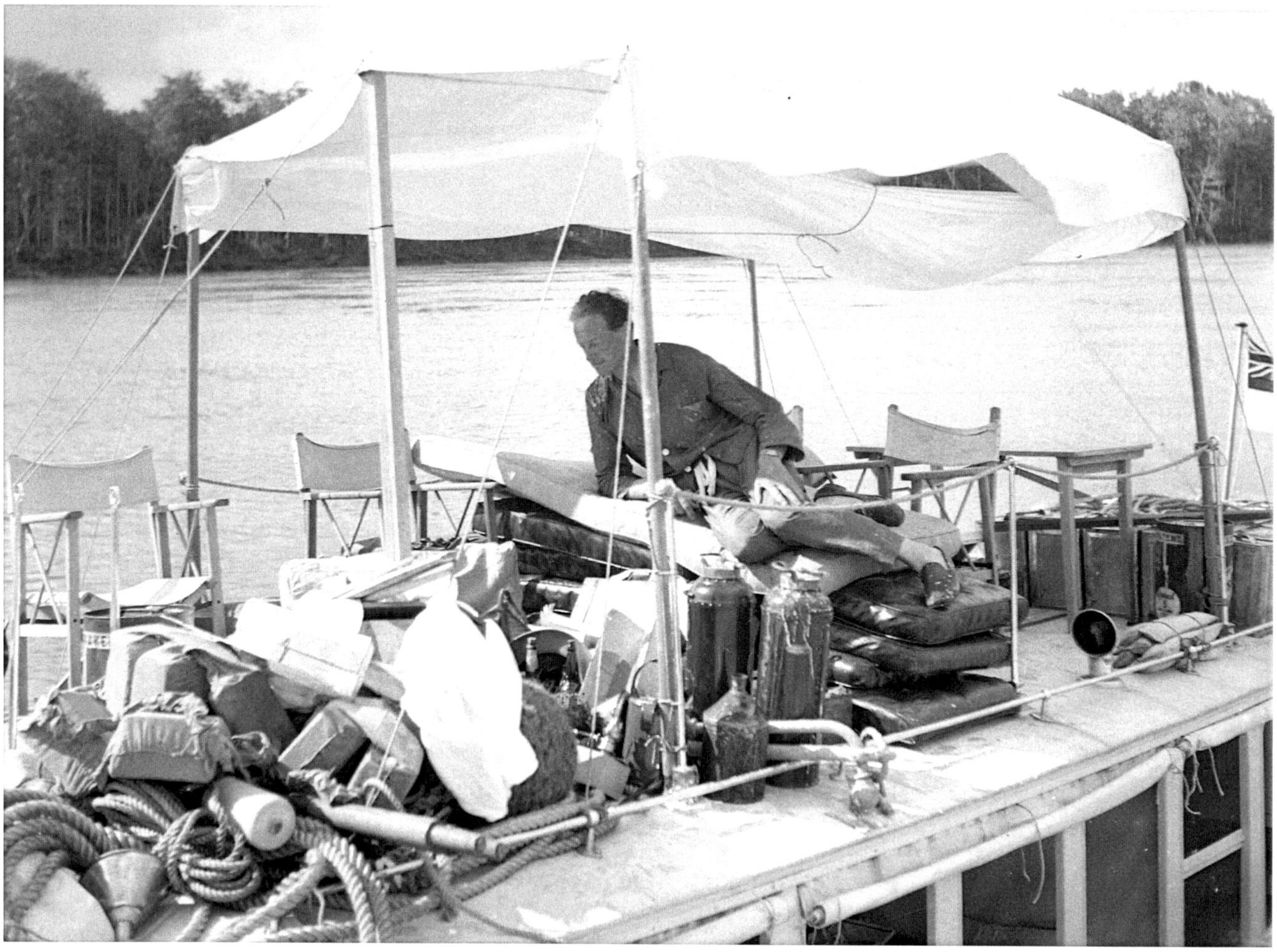

Figure 9 Lord Moyne on the *Aura*, 1935. Photograph taken by Lady Delves Broughton. RAI 400.36767

Figure 10 Photograph taken by Lord Moyne on the Eilanden River in 1929 and reproduced in 'Travels WEG' album

Figure 11 'Vera Broughton taking a photograph', Borneo 1935. Photographer unknown. RAI 400.38764

Figure 12 Lady Delves Broughton game hunting in Africa in February 1935. Photographer unknown. RAI 400.38411

Figure 13 Lady Delves Broughton with marlin catch in February 1935, reproduced in Eastern Cruise 1934/35 album. Photographer unknown

number of public offices during the 1930s (Bond and Robbins 1987; Miley 2008). Therefore, in 1929 at the age of 49, he now had plenty of time to devote to his other interests that had lain dormant since leaving school.

Moyne possessed considerable wealth, a critical factor in his pursuit of adventure. As commentators on first contact expeditions have noted: 'The scarcer these places became, the higher their ostensible value, the more expensive they became to find, the more sponsors of wealth were needed to undertake the expedition' (Bell, Brown and Gordon 2013: 3). Proper finances were vitally important. Ten years earlier the Royal Geographical Society had sponsored the yacht *St George* to undertake scientific research in the South Pacific. The RGS hoped to recoup its costs from a film of the cruise but their hopes came to nothing. As they reflected: 'these hopes have not been justified, and it is extremely unlikely that a similar cruise can ever be attempted' (Douglas and Johnson 1926: xi). But Moyne proved them wrong. He was under no such commercial or financial pressure and therefore had no need of sponsors and could follow his own agenda unimpeded by others. He was able to finance six trips to the Pacific from 1929 until 1936. Three of these voyages included visits to the south coast of Papua in 1929, 1935 and 1936. The only extant record of his first trip in 1929 is provided by his photographic album 'Travels WEG' (**Fig. 10**) in addition to the collection of 88 artefacts that he gave to the British Museum in 1934. His notes of the visit were destroyed when his yacht MY *Roussalka* sank off the west coast of Ireland in August 1933, so no record survives of his 1929 itinerary.

Lady Vera Delves Broughton (1894–1968) relished game hunting, especially in Africa, and was known for shooting lions, elephants and rhinoceros, as well as hunting fish like marlin and shark (**Figs 11–13**). A *Dictionary of National Biography* entry states: 'Vera Broughton was a hard, pleasure-loving woman whose passion for big-game hunting first took [her] to Kenya in 1919–20' (Davenport Hines 2004: 1026). As Moyne remarked, 'Vera has for years chased strange people and rare animals with her camera' (Moyne 1936a: 6). He might have added, 'but also with her rifle in hand'. She photographed wherever she went and constructed some 12 or more albums of her adventures, each carefully captioned with details of location. She recorded through photographs both the second trip to the Pacific in 1934/5 and the third in 1935/6. She created a bespoke album of the Walkabout trip for Lord Elveden, Moyne's nephew, who was a fellow traveller on the 1936 trip (**Fig. 14**), giving his contribution to the story special prominence. Delves Broughton also published pictures of the 1934 trip in *The Times* on 2 and 23 May 1935, and her photographs illustrated Moyne's *Walkabout* (Moyne 1936a).

Other passengers in 1935/6 included Clementine Churchill (Winston Churchill's wife); Captain and Mrs Edward Orlando Kellett (who had just completed a motor tour from London to Calcutta via Afghanistan and was also a big game hunter); Moyne's cousin, Lee and Mrs Guinness;

Figure 14 Viscount Elveden bailing out the launches, 1936. Photograph taken by Lady Delves Broughton. RAI 400.36728

Figure 15 Rosamond Delves Broughton, 1936. Photograph taken by Lady Delves Broughton. RAI 400.38726

and Terence Philip, an art dealer. The trip in 1935/6 was more ambitious in scope, with zoological exploration as a further objective, for which amateur zoologists Anthony and Alvida Chaplin were responsible, assisted by Keeper Reg Lanworn of the reptile house at London Zoo who took Komodo dragons back to London with him. Moyne's nephew, Arthur Onslow Edward Guinness (Lord Elveden), 'a tall well-built young man' (Singapore Free Press 1935: 10), was also a member of the group and he took a seven-reel cine-film of the voyage.

Vera Delves Broughton's 19-year-old daughter Rosamond also travelled with the party in 1935/6 and, as will become evident, became a major participant in exchanges with the local people (**Fig. 15**). The group was also accompanied on the third trip by a professional photographer, Arthur Pereira, Honorary Secretary of the Royal Photographic Society, who had previously filmed in Africa. Copies of his photographs of the trip were given to Cambridge University Museum of Archaeology and Ethnology as detailed in a letter from Moyne to the curator, Louis Clarke: 'The photographs of natives were taken by Lady Broughton who is at the moment away from London. As however we had a professional photographer on board who took photographs of almost all the same subjects that she did, I think it will suit your purpose equally well if I get you a set of his' (Moyne 1936e).

The *Rosaura*: mother ship, laboratory and ark

For Moyne a ship offered the perfect solution that enabled him to have an exciting but also luxurious adventure as well as to facilitate his collecton of artefacts, animals and birds and allow him to take photographs of local people. For the modern reader such a conflation might appear problematic. But Moyne was quite content to bring home live and dead specimens of mammals, birds, amphibians and reptiles, as well as human skulls. All were worth study in their own right and were accorded equal significance. All had a place in the ark. Sometimes categories blurred into a single image as in **Figure 16** where the photograph captures the person, the artefact and, inferentially, its origin. The dagger displayed in the photograph (**Fig. 17**) now resides in the British Museum.

Figure 16 Kampong River natives with bone dagger of crocodile jaw bone, 1936, reproduced as Plate 11 in *Walkabout* (Moyne 1936a). Photograph taken by Lady Delves Broughton. British Museum, Oc,B28.10

Figure 17 Bone dagger made from crocodile jaw bone collected by Lord Moyne in 1936 (as seen in Fig. 16). British Museum, Oc1936,0720.229

Figure 18 Swimming bath on the *Rosaura*, reproduced in Eastern Cruise 1934/35 album. Photograph taken by Lady Delves Broughton

Figure 19 The *Rosaura*, 1935, reproduced as Plate 2 in *Walkabout* (Moyne 1936a). Photograph taken by Lady Delves Broughton

Moyne's yacht played an important facilitating role in the expedition. The *Rosaura*, like the *Arpha* and *Roussalka* previously owned by Moyne, had been purchased from Southern Railways. The *Rosaura* began life in 1905 as the SS *Dieppe*, a cross-channel ferry, which served in the First World War as a troop ship and, after decommissioning, resumed carrying passengers until 1933, when Moyne bought it. Moyne described it as 'a gallant old ship of 700 tons net which, after battling with the choppy seas between Newhaven and Dieppe for nearly thirty years, had been discarded as too small for the demands of modern traffic' (Moyne 1936a: 10). His recollection was inaccurate in one important respect, in that the ship was twice the tonnage that he recalled. Moyne bought the ship a month after his previous yacht the MY *Roussalka* sank off the Irish coast. He refitted it as a private yacht, and 'the interior [was] furnished in the modern style. An extensive library, a phonograph and a wireless set, a special sports deck, and a swimming bath [**Fig. 18**] were among the comforts provided for the yacht's passengers' (*Sydney Morning Herald*, 7 February 1935, 11).

The ship was renamed the *Rosaura* (**Fig. 19**), taking the name of Moyne's then 13 year-old daughter. Moyne's early guests included the Prince of Wales and Wallis Simpson in 1933, and Winston and Clementine Churchill on a cruise to the Mediterranean in 1934. The yacht acquired two powerful 36-ft launches, named respectively the *Rose* (**Fig. 20**) and the *Aura*, brought along specifically to explore the river systems of Papua. In order to enter narrow creeks and visit the river banks Moyne and his party used dinghies (**Fig. 21**). This combination of vessels gave Moyne's party exceptional opportunities. The size of the *Rosaura* meant that they could sail independently around the world and stop wherever they chose without need of berth or docks. The ship's echo-sounding equipment was used to avoid the constantly shifting mud banks at the river mouths and prevent the danger of running aground.

The ship carried all the equipment needed for the six-month trip and provided accommodation for the extensive menagerie of captured wildlife, including mammals, birds and reptiles, as well as the hundreds of artefacts obtained from local people. Some of these objects were very large and delicate and would have been extremely difficult to export without this facility. Crucially, the ship also afforded repair facilities for the launches when they were damaged by submerged logs in the rivers as occurred on the very first day of exploring the Bloemen River. The launches

Figure 20 The launch *Rose*. Note the dinghies tied up at the stern. Photograph taken by Lady Delves Broughton. RAI 400.36791

Figure 21 Lord Moyne in dinghy, 1935. Photograph taken by Lady Delves Broughton. RAI 400.36762

were vital to the enterprise. As Moyne noted, 'we had to leave the ship from ten to fifteen miles out from the coast, almost out of sight of the low-lying land. We lay generally in a heavy ground swell which made it difficult to either lower or pick up our launches without crashing them against the sides of the ship' (Moyne 1936a: 20). The launches enabled the explorers to venture far up the river system, travelling for three days and 40 miles up the Bloemen River, and 55 miles up the Eilanden and Kampong rivers. Their powerful motors were a source of alarm to the locals. As Moyne noted: 'they were much afraid of our launches and ran to cover whenever we started the engines' (Moyne 1936a: 34). To make effective contact and to engage with local people the travellers had to move to the dinghies. So, all three types of craft played their respective part in exploring a bewilderingly vast, but simultaneously monotonous muddy brown environment. However, unlike most regular explorers, passengers on the *Rosaura* could retire from a day's outing in the mud to the luxury of the cruise ship with its comfort and safety. Clementine Churchill reflected on her return from an outing:

> We were all drenched from top to toe. I thought the launch would capsize (quite impossible I'm told). So in spite of the soaking wet I took off my mackintosh and shoes so as to be free if anything went wrong. But of course it didn't. But Oh was I glad when we got alongside of the yacht. Six miserable dripping creatures climbed up the ladder and in spite of a temperature of 86 degrees fell into hot baths.
> (Churchill 1935: 27)

The prime objective of Moyne's Pacific cruises was ethnological, but his interests also included physiology and in particular the study of human crania. Collecting skulls became a major part of his 'scientific measurement project'. Moyne also had a genuine interest in social anthropology. He prepared for his trips by reading A.F.R. Wollaston's *Pygmies and Papuans*, which recounted the hardship that the author had endured attempting to conquer the Jayawijaya Mountains at the headwaters of the Utakwa (currently known as the Otakwa) River in the Mimika district to the west of Asmat. Moyne was evidently not put off by Wollaston's description of the Papuan south coast as 'the most dreary and forbidding country I have ever seen. There is nothing beautiful in it, nothing of romance, nothing to stir one's imagination in the least, but altogether an utterly soul-destroying land' (Wollaston 1933: 102). This was precisely the challenge that Moyne would relish. Moyne also read Julian Huxley and A.C. Haddon's *We Europeans* and was particularly struck by their assertion that

> as far as European populations are concerned, nothing in the nature of 'pure race' in the biological sense has any real existence... I was anxious to see whether the same variety of type exists among the native peoples of New Guinea. Enmity between the little communities must have continued there for very long periods of time, judging by the number of mutually incomprehensible languages which exist side by side within quite small areas. It would be interesting to see whether such long isolation had brought about the development of more uniform local types.
> (Moyne 1936a: 5)

He also sought advice from H.J. Braunholtz at the British Museum on which places to visit. Braunholtz, as an ethnographer associated with the Royal Anthropological Institute, was familiar with the Dutch *Nova Guinea* series of publications of 1923 that had a 'scientific' interest in anthropometric measurement. These were themes that Moyne would follow enthusiastically. But the whole exploratory exercise was suffused by a spirit of what would later be called 'salvage ethnography' or, perhaps more bluntly, the search for the primitive. Moyne expressed this clearly in the introduction to his book: 'Some of us had never travelled off the beaten track and the younger generation were especially anxious to see cannibals and other interesting survivals before they vanish from the world' (Moyne 1936a: 6). Clementine Churchill's excitement on arrival on the Eilanden River was expressed in a letter home to her husband Winston: 'This is the genuine article! – uncharted seas, unexplored territory, stark naked savages' (Churchill 1935: 24).

Moyne explained his motivation for the 1936 visit in similar though less colourful terms:

> Owing to the quickening of travel and communication, civilization is becoming uniform and monotonous. In an effort to get beyond the regions of semi-civilized natives in cheap pyjamas or badly fitting European clothes and to find human and animal life in primitive conditions, we made a cruise in my yacht Rosaura early this year to the Dutch East Indies and some of the islands near the east and south-east of New Guinea.
> (Moyne 1935: 17)

Neither of Moyne's trips to the Pacific was lengthy. The 1934/5 cruise lasted four months (December to April), the 1935/6 one six months (November to April). This meant that individual ports of call seldom lasted more than a week, often considerably less. This was certainly the case for both stops in Asmat. Moyne was keenly aware of this limitation. He wrote to Henry Balfour at the Pitt Rivers Museum: 'One difficulty is the very large area which we covered and the superficial views to which we were for this reason limited even if we had been experts which we certainly were not' (Moyne 1936c).

The record of the voyages, both written and photographic, is uneven. This undoubtedly reflects Moyne's penchant for the exotic and why he paid special attention to the south coast of Dutch New Guinea, and the territory inhabited by the Asmat people. He selected this area for two reasons. First was remoteness. In 1935 Moyne called in on the Dutch Resident of the Moluccas in Amboina on his way to New Guinea. Moyne reported to the Resident: 'I found in the six years since a previous visit a great development in communications and government' and asked the Resident 'where natives living under primitive conditions could still be found' (Moyne 1935a). The Resident directed Moyne to the Asmat area and warned that there was no effective government there. Neither the Resident nor any of his officials had ventured there and he warned Moyne that the local people were dangerous. This was just the sort of place that Moyne relished, where colonial authority had not yet been established and where direct and unmediated contact with local people could take place; in short, a pre-colonial setting where mutual expectations had not solidified into definite patterns of behaviour. As Clementine Churchill wrote: 'Dr Hage (the Dutch Resident at Amboina) ... told us

Figure 22 Exchange on Eilanden River 1935, reproduced in Eastern Cruise 1934/35 album. Photograph taken by Lady Delves Broughton

Figure 23 'Lovely girl', Eilanden River, 1936. Photograph taken by Lady Delves Broughton. RAI 400.37737

Figure 24 'Kampong River Native', 1936, reproduced as Plate 13 in *Walkabout* (Moyne 1936a). Photograph taken by Lady Delves Broughton. British Museum, Oc,B94.44

that there were no Dutch officials in N.G. except at Merauke and that for 1000 miles of the south coast it is practically unexplored and unknown. Walter of course decided upon the most savage and unapproachable spot!' (Churchill 1935). Moyne noted parenthetically that the art of this region 'was entirely unrepresented in the British Museum. I therefore wished to collect further examples of native handicraft from here' (Moyne 1936a: 4). The decision to concentrate efforts in this location stemmed from his preliminary visit in 1929. As he recorded:

> I found these stark naked cannibals intensely interesting. Living in swamps with no metal weapons or tools and where even stone is a valuable commodity only to be obtained from the distant foothills by long journeys through the territories of hostile neighbours, they none the less produce highly decorative carved and painted woodwork.
> (Moyne 1936a: 3)

The account of this part of the 1936 voyage is far more detailed than any other, consisting of 27 pages of text and 13 pages of plates. Moyne recognised the importance of this locale for his tale, noting 'although it deals with other countries than New Guinea, the only part which is likely to be of any interest is concerned with that region' (Moyne 1936b). A similar concentration on the area and people is to be found in Delves Broughton's photographic archive housed at the Royal Anthropological Institute. Apart from wildlife hunting scenes in Africa, Delves Broughton's imagery consistently privileges the Asmat region. Two other albums compiled by Delves Broughton survive, the first entitled 'Eastern Cruise 1934/35' and the second 'Eastern Trip 1935–36'. They both give prominence to the visit to Asmat. The same is true for the 16mm film reels taken by Arthur Elveden. Two of the seven reels taken during the Walkabout voyage are devoted to the Asmat. There was clearly a special interest for the adventurers in the Asmat people.

The hosts

One of the first observations that should be made is that this series of photographs and the accompanying captions are made with the explicit agenda of capturing the 'culture of the Stone Age – often without the stone' (Moyne 1936a: 34), alongside a determination to explore the most remote locations on earth. It requires some patience to place the images of the Asmat within the chronology of *Walkabout*. In the book Asmat images from 1935 are juxtaposed with those from 1936. The Delves Broughton albums help create a timeline but it is easier to deal with the photographs by location rather than date. The inhabitants of the Eilanden and Kampong rivers are shown as active and equal partners in the exchanges with Moyne's party. Three figures stand out for their symbolic presence (**Figs 22–4**) and they appear in several photographs and in the first two cases over different years. The bearer of the shield in **Figure 22** appears in both 1929 and 1935. 'Lovely girl' is similarly photographed in 1935 and 1936 (see **Fig. 57**). Their regular presence is important. Each of these three actors shown above appears in numerous photographs underlining their continuous presence and each play a central role in the unfolding picture of Asmat life on the rivers.

Although they were unable to communicate through language, both the Walkabout photographers and their subjects contrived displays of paddling before a stationary camera. Reality could have been very different, with no staged poses, and active protest against visual intrusion. Both parties had potential to employ weapons in pursuit of their aims. In fact, only occasionally does weaponry appear in the photographs offering a hint at the dangers faced by both groups, as is apparent in **Figure 25**.

Captions beneath the plates of *Walkabout* were designed usually to provide background information about the image. But on at least two occasions Moyne's (or perhaps Moyne's and Delves Broughton's) captions invite the reader into the action through the medium of an interrogative framework. The *Walkabout* Plate 10 is captioned 'Friendly or unfriendly? Natives of the Kampong River. Note the 15-foot paddle spear' (**Fig. 67**) and similarly Plate 16's caption reads 'Hero or victim? A pile of broken skulls were found behind this broken shield which stood defiantly at the entrance to the hut' (**Fig. 39**). The texts are open to several readings. They can be seen as reflective, echoing the uncertainty that attended the explorers' own engagement with the scene. Alternatively they can be seen as pedagogic, challenging the viewer to reconsider their expectations and prejudices, something the explorers had learnt to do. Or perhaps the captions act as a marker of the explorers' sense of their heroic achievement. The captions certainly suggest that

Figure 25 The tender *Aura* at the meeting of the Kampong and Eilanden rivers, 1935, Photograph taken by Lady Delves Broughton. RAI 400.36803

mystery and uncertainty were active elements in the fragile and tenuous relationships between hosts and visitors. What the Asmat made of the camera or its operation is not recorded. It is not likely that they would have seen the photographs taken, as Delves Broughton did not develop photographs on board until the next adventure on the *Rosaura*, chronicled in Moyne's *Atlantic Circle*.

The images also introduce a third set of actors beside the photographer and the photographed: the addressee of the image. There is a range of potential readers of these Asmat portraits. The most immediate were members of the Guinness and Delves Broughton families who have remained custodians of the photographic albums. The captions were mostly directed to these privileged viewers. The photographs and artefacts were also put on public display shortly after the conclusion of the 1936 expedition at an exhibition at the Guinness residence in London that was held as a fundraising event for the Royal Anthropological Institute with the intention of reaching a more academic audience (**Fig. 26**).

A more general audience were newspaper and magazine readers both in Britain (Delves Broughton 1935a and 1935b; Moyne 1935a, 1935b, 1936b) and throughout the Empire (*Singapore Free Press* 1935; *Sydney Morning Herald* 1935). The 1934/5 voyage was extensively covered in *The Times* newspaper with contributions from both Vera Delves Broughton and Lord Moyne followed up with an article 'Islands of the Western Pacific' in *Country Life* in June that year (Moyne 1935b). Perhaps public interest in Moyne's activities waned after such exposure, as the 1935/6 visit was only reported in *The Daily Telegraph* in June 1936. All of these audiences were the targets of Moyne's travelogue *Walkabout*. Finally, in a more general sense, these Asmat portraits were intended as a record of what the writer and photographer were sure were a people doomed to be swept into history and out of their traditional lifestyle. And yet these Asmat portraits are still vibrant. To this day they remain defiantly commanding images of people who were confident in their ability to deal with visitors from outside the swamp, unadorned with any sense of nostalgia.

The photographs and their focus

The Asmat photographs should be considered not just as evidence, but as perceptions constructed by their authors. They offer a significant contribution to photographic history, and in this context we can also acknowledge that at the time they were taken there was also the development of what Max Quanchi has called 'the Papuan Gallery', particularly in the adjacent Australian colonial territories of Papua and New Guinea. As Quanchi explained: 'Public understanding of Papua was not based on seeing everything that circulated in the public domain, but only a selective, small, often repeated, set of images that evolved from an

Figure 26 'Shields from Eilanden River', on display in an exhibition of specimens and photographs from *Rosaura's* cruise held at 10 Grosvenor Place London, 1936, for the Royal Anthropological Institute. Photograph taken by D.J Kunst, Royal Colonial Institute, Amsterdam. British Museum Oc,B101.44

iconographic imperative that reduced the totality of experience in Papua to a few summative images. This reduction involved sending home photographs which were representative, but exotic and of enough interest to attract favourable dinner party comment or the attention of journal, newspaper, serial encyclopedia and magazine editors' (Quanchi 2007: 22). At most a set of ten interesting photographs was sufficient to fill the gallery. But, as Quanchi remarked, the reading public had become more sophisticated and was no longer content with 'the exotic, the erotic and wild ... they demanded intimate portraits, jungle views and frontier vignettes' (Quanchi 2007: 47). To what extent are what I will call, for simplicity's sake, the 'Walkabout photographs' part of this Papuan Gallery? As I hope to argue in my discussion of the whole project, the Walkabout photographs do not fit neatly into Quanchi's picture. First, they do not contribute to the official colonial history of West Papua. They come from a moment before any 'Asmat Gallery' could be established. Neither were they constructed with a commercial intent. They have a remarkably narrow field of focus but in their entirety form a considerable body of work. The 1929 album includes 16 photographs taken on the Eilanden River. The 1935 album has 79 photographs. The third made during the Walkabout Cruise in 1936 is the largest with 379 images, with mostly four images to a page. In addition the donation made by Moyne to the RAI consists of 1,379 prints, while Lady Delves Broughton's suitcase, also donated to the RAI, contains 287 4' x 3' glass negatives, 929 celluloid negatives, as well as two 100' reels of 16mm and one 400' reel also of 16mm. Lord Elveden's 16mm film of the Walkabout tour adds another seven reels to the story of the whole tour. This makes for the largest corpus of visual material created before the advent of proper colonial presence in the region.

The status of the photographs, albums and film is enhanced by their number and close attention to detail. No other photographs of the area were published from 1936 until the Missionaries of the Sacred Heart and the Dutch government established a post in Agats in 1953 (Ohoroiwin 2011), well after the Japanese invasion of 1942 had been defeated in 1945. Paradoxically, it was only when the Dutch realised that their days as a colonial presence were drawing to a close in 1960 that any systematic study of the people and geography of Papua took place (van Duuren and Vink 2011: 153). The new research was undertaken under the auspices of the Colonial Institute but the results never returned to Papua. After the Dutch left in 1963 only missionaries stayed on to document the new world under Indonesian rule.

However, they only published in religious journals (Zegwaard 1952, 1955). There was, however, a sudden spurt of interest in the area just as the colonial administration was drawing to a close. In 1959 a French film crew made a widely viewed film about the region entitled *The Sky Above, the Mud Below* which won a prize at the Cannes Film Festival (Saulnier 1963). The Museum of Primitive Art in New York under the direction of Robert Goldwater took an interest in Asmat art (Stanley forthcoming) and one of its trustees, Michael Rockefeller, made a series of photographs in the villages in 1961 which were published in his posthumous account (Rockefeller 1967). This in turn led to *National Geographic Magazine* articles in 1968 and 1969 and a further feature article in 1996 (Stanley 2012: 171–9). Further photographic studies have followed right up to the present day (Irwandi 2014; Villevoye 2008).

Although most of these later photographers saw the illustrations in *Walkabout* none have had access to the archive of still and moving imagery that the book drew upon. Quanchi (2007: 61), writing about Papua generally, reminds us that a huge proportion of the historic photographs taken were lost or discarded, so those that remain have additional authority. Therefore, the extant Walkabout albums shown here provide a rare and vital picture of Asmat before external forces impacted on the people and the region. These photographs form a remarkable body of closely focused work. However, certain preoccupations of the photographers shape the record and provide a particular lens through which the territory and people can be seen. As the next chapter will show, early contact was particularly closely documented, as were special features of local buildings, canoes and rowing, and the apparent anomaly of senior women among the warriors. These were all themes that fascinated Moyne and his companions.

To what extent do these photographs reinforce Moyne's claim to have struck up a genuine friendship with his hosts? The introduction by Roche in 1929 served to make their acquaintance and Moyne used his two subsequent visits to cement this relationship. Despite early hesitancy and anxiety on both sides, they enjoyed their meetings as the photographs in the next chapters will display. Crucially, although both had weapons to call upon, neither party resorted to using them. This was in marked difference to all previous recorded meetings between Europeans and the Asmat. The contrast was even starker with the well-known contemporary explorer, Michael Leahy, who was opening up the New Guinea Highlands in the 1930s. Leahy regularly resorted to shooting local people who opposed him (Connolly and Anderson 1987). Careful management by both Asmat hosts and Moyne's party achieved a real rapport as the imagery demonstrates and no one suffered in the complex sets of negotiations of mutual exchange throughout the period.

Chapter 2
Making Contact

First sight

The visual record of Moyne's first visit to Asmat in 1929 looks similar to the earlier Dutch photographs. Canoes came to explore the ship and both parties are seen meeting at close quarters (see **Fig. 8**). But there is one new development in Moyne's photographs – white shirts worn by two of the rowers (**Fig. 27**).

Moyne explained this to Braunholtz in a letter in 1934, which also commented on the quality of the 1929 images: 'I am afraid the photographs are very poor as the negatives got spoilt by the damp before they could be developed. No clothing of any kind was possessed by the natives and the white shirts which appear in some of the photographs were obtained from members of my crew in exchange for birds of paradise' (Moyne 1934). Therefore exchange relationships were established from the start. What is also interesting is that although the picture quality is poor, an individual can be identified from the 1929 visit (**Fig. 28**), who features in later visits as the first host identified bearing a shield in 1935 (see **Fig. 22**) who appears again in 1936 (**Fig. 29**).

In 1929, thanks to the benefit of Roche's experience, Moyne had gained a good sense of the geography of the region. The opening sequence of the 1936 Walkabout film shows the main rivers visited, though not the full extent of each trip (**Fig. 30**). The only river not indicated on this map is the Doyussi which lies immediately to the south of the Kampong. Moyne had visited all of these rivers in his 1929 tour that covered 200 miles, except for the most westerly, the Bloemen River. When he returned to Asmat in January 1936 the absence of people on the Bloemen River proved both a disappointment and an opportunity, as well as an ethical challenge. Despite travelling for three days and some 40 miles he met no local people. The villages were deserted and Moyne speculated that this did not necessarily mean that there were no people around, but that they were keeping out of the way, particularly from the loud engines reverberating

Figure 27 Photograph taken by Lord Moyne in 1929 and reproduced in 'Travels WEG' album

Figure 28 Photograph taken by Lord Moyne on the Eilanden River in 1929 and reproduced in 'Travels WEG' album

Figure 29 Scene on the Eilanden River, 1936, still from Walkabout film taken by Viscount Elveden

across the waterways. Moyne was convinced that the inhabitants were slipping down side channels away from the main river and decided to explore some of the villages, most of which were seasonal bivouacs in a poor state of repair. Moyne's exploration of these deserted villages form a central theme in the visual record.

Deserted villages

One particular village was larger than the others and consisted of about 20 houses along the river's edge. These were constructed on wooden piles, the largest with a double roof (**Fig. 31**). The party spent some time looking around the village peering into every house. Moyne found access difficult. He noted: 'the vegetation in and under the houses was higher than our heads and it was a very creepy experience to force our way through the tangle into the houses. The interiors were so dark that it was almost impossible to see what was hidden there and the difficulty of the search was the greater as we were continually falling through the rotten woodwork of the floors into the muddy swamp beneath' (Moyne 1936a: 26). Three houses provided a range of artefacts that were collected.

In the first, the one with the double roof (**Fig. 32**), the visitors observed that 'two poles towards each end of the row of uprights supporting the gallery which ran along the front towards the river were painted and carved to represent male and female figures respectively and each had a curious fretwork projection tilted upwards from about the position of the breastbone' (Moyne 1936a: 25). As the visitors could not discern their function the figures were described as 'effigies' and their location was identified as an effigy house. Moyne hacked the pole down (as seen on the Walkabout film) and bore it away (**Fig. 33**). It joined a display on the *Rosaura* (**Fig. 34**) and was later reproduced in an article published by Braunholtz (**Fig. 35**). A further house revealed a pair of painted posts and in the third was a pair of shields. In his 1936 article Braunholtz explained the provenance of the items shown in **Figure 35** which was a reconstruction of the earlier montage in **Figure 34**:

> The two taller posts, representing a man and woman with projections carved in openwork, were cut off the tops of poles, standing at each end of a row of uprights supporting the front platform of the largest house. The two outer poles were taken from the tops of two beams lying among the rafters of another house. They are new and had apparently never been erected. The shields, with handles behind, are cut from solid wood. (Braunholtz 1936: 96)

The village was deserted and there was evidence that it had been abandoned in haste with objects of daily life left

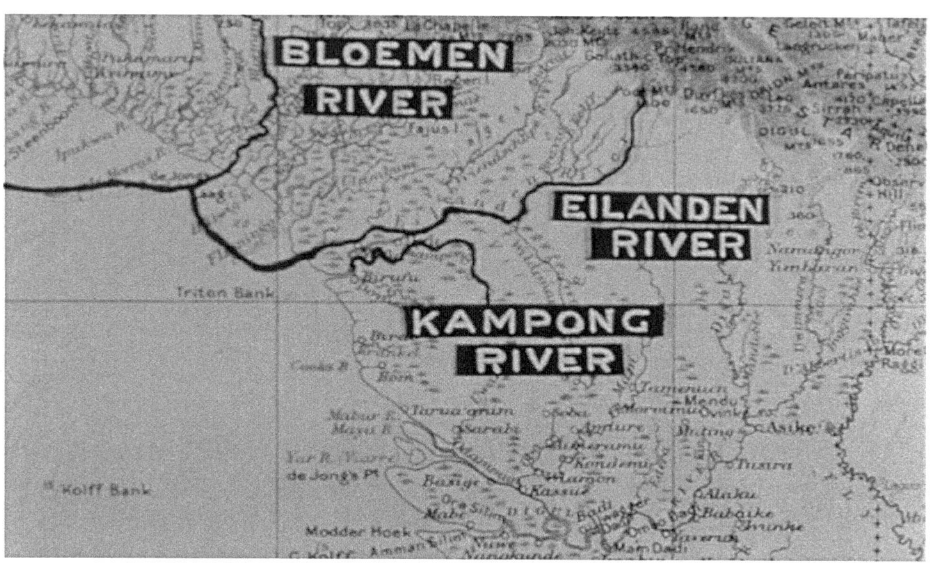

Figure 30 Opening sequence of the 1936 Walkabout film taken by Viscount Elveden showing the main rivers visited by Lord Moyne

Figure 31 Structure in forest along the Eilanden River, 1936. Photograph taken by A. Pereira. RAI 400.07188

Figure 32 Deserted village on the Bloemen River, 1936. Photograph taken by Lady Delves Broughton. British Museum, Oc,B28.3

Figure 33 Lord Moyne holding ceremonial pole, 1936. Photograph taken by Lady Delves Broughton. RAI 400.36751

Figure 34 'Objects collected from abandoned village on the Bloemen River', 1936. Photograph taken by Lady Delves Broughton. RAI 400.36803

Figure 35 'Wooden shields and house posts', reproduced as Plate H, Fig. 1 in Braunholtz 1936. Photograph taken by Lady Delves Broughton. RAI 400.36804

scattered around. There were drums, sago-beaters, axe-heads and ceremonial masks stored in the rafters. There were also several pig's jaw bones, which were systematically collected as shown in **Figure 36**.

There was more evidence of Asmat occupation throughout the deserted villages, with strings of 27 skulls hung from the rafters. Most of these seem to have been collected by the visitors as **Figures 37–8** demonstrate. Moyne speculated that the presence of the skulls meant that the village had been attacked, as no native of this area would voluntarily leave skulls or other valued possessions behind them. Moyne made collecting skulls an important

Figure 36 Pig jaw bones from the Bloemen River, 1936. Photograph taken by Lady Delves Broughton. RAI 400.39113

Figure 37 Loading skulls from an abandoned village onto a dinghy, 1936, reproduced in Eastern Trip 1935–36 album. Photograph taken by Lady Delves Broughton

Figure 38 Viscount Elveden, Rosamond Delves Broughton and crew member with human skulls on Bloemen River, 1936. Photograph taken by Lady Delves Broughton. RAI 400.36805

part of his scientific programme and had arranged for his collection to be examined by anatomists at the Royal College of Surgeons on his return. Dr A.J.E. Cave of the Royal College of Surgeons studied these skulls devoting 15 pages in an appendix of 60 pages in *Walkabout* to the analysis of the variety of types that could be found on the Bloemen River. Therefore skulls came to provide a leitmotif to both the written account and the imagery of the expedition.

Moyne was aware of the ethical issues he and his party faced in exploring deserted habitations. There was no one to grant permission for them to take away the items they valued, nor were they able to pay for what they took. Moyne devised a rather crude rule-of-thumb rationale: 'Where we took bones or weapons from villages showing signs of present or recent occupation we were always careful to leave as payment a bush knife or some other article of value to the natives.' But, Moyne continued: 'In the case of the abandoned settlement on the Bloemen, however, we had been puzzled to know how to make payment, as vegetation and the rotten state of the floors showed that no one could have been in the houses for many months' (Moyne 1936a: 40). In other words, no payment was made for the removal of items if the visitors judged the encampment abandoned.

Moyne's confusion about the status of objects that he saw and obtained is captured nicely in the photograph used to illustrate his visit to the Kampong River (**Fig. 39**). Even in a large new village in good repair there were no inhabitants. He recorded, 'in front of one of the larger houses we found a broken shield tied to a spear which had been driven into the ground and fixed under the eaves of the house by the haft of a sago axe. The shield was decorated with a bunch of palm fibre and five broken skulls were lying behind' (Moyne 1936a: 39). His frustration in trying to understand its meaning can be clearly discerned by the caption that he gave this photograph in Plate 16 in *Walkabout*.

Moyne interpreted the shield's placement as a tabu or stern warning to strangers to keep away. So he refrained from collecting it and moved on to places that he had previously visited where he expected a more welcoming reception.

Rowing prowess

As a champion sculler himself, Moyne was quick to note the superb rowing skills of the Asmat from his first sighting of them approaching him on the Eilanden and Kampong rivers. He commented: 'the rhythm and speed of the crews was amazing and I judged them to be moving at a speed of about ten knots' (Moyne 1936a: 42). Moyne also appreciated the excellent balance required to row from a standing position, made the more difficult by the shallow draught and narrow girth of the dugout canoes. The dimensions of the canoe were captured clearly in **Figure 40**. What is noticeable is that there are no thwarts or seats on which to balance. The stability of the craft could only be maintained by each rower compensating for his companions' movements, a feat easier to accomplish when travelling at speed but extremely tricky when manoeuvring at close quarters in strong currents, especially in confined spaces. Both Delves Broughton and Pereira attempted to capture the aesthetic of the activity. In **Figure 41** Delves Broughton captured a real sense of speed and agility in the canoe accelerating from the river bank. The point at which the front rower's arm meets the head of the paddle acts as a dynamic fulcrum providing forward impetus whilst sustaining the rower's upright posture. The back of the copy of the photograph held in Cambridge is annotated by Delves Broughton with further explanatory text: 'Canoe paddles often serve a double purpose having a pointed end for use as a spear in river fighting. The decoration of cassowary feathers.'

What neither of the photographs caught is the special Asmat high-speed paddling that is traditionally done with

Figure 39 'Hero or victim? A pile of broken skulls were found behind this broken shield which stood defiantly at the entrance to the hut', 1936, reproduced as Plate 16 in *Walkabout* (Moyne 1936a). Photograph taken by Lady Delves Broughton. RAI Eastern Trip

Figure 40 Men in canoes, Eilanden River, 1936. Photograph taken by A. Pereira. RAI 7193

Figure 41 Men in canoes, Kampong River, 1936. Photograph taken by Lady Delves Broughton. British Museum, Oc,B94.28

Figure 42 Page from Eastern Trip 1935–36 album showing images of exchange on the Kampong River, 1936. Photographs taken by Lady Delves Broughton

the rowers standing not on the floor of the canoe but perching on the gunwales. This delicate stance provides extra thrust though it is achieved at the rowers' expense of greater fatigue, while balanced on such narrow ledges.

One way that Delves Broughton captured movement was to place images in sequence, and one of the most successful means of doing so was through the composition of the album page, of which **Figure 42** is a good example.

The top two images offer a pan from right to left, showing the canoe in the distance moving briskly, creating a composite panorama. The bottom left image contrasts energetic paddling by the distant canoe with the front one coming to rest whilst the bottom right image shows all three canoes at rest. This last image contains an additional feature that attracted Delves Broughton's eye: geometric form. All of the rowers have their paddles across their bodies, mostly over their right shoulder. The most prominent rower, however, holds his paddle at rest over his left shoulder and brandishes a spear towards the camera in the opposite direction. The rower is therefore at the centre of a St Andrew's cross figuration, giving him further prominence. These are visual compositions that Delves Broughton often sought. **Figure 44** is perhaps the most majestic composition in the series with its predecessor study shown as **Figure 43**.

Here Delves Broughton has composed two fairly static images that contrast the stark diagonals of the paddles with the feathery softness of the nipa palms at the river's edge. The river surface and palm leaves are ruffled by the wind whilst the men remain at rest in the centre of the field of vision. Elsewhere in this series taken on the Eilanden River,

Figure 43 (left) Men in canoes on the North Eilanden River, 1936. Photograph taken by Lady Delves Broughton. RAI 400.37724

Figure 44 (below) Men in canoes on the North Eilanden River, 1936, reproduced in Eastern Trip 1935–36 album. Photograph taken by Lady Delves Broughton

Figure 45 Men in canoes on the Eilanden River, 1936. Photograph taken by A. Pereira. RAI 400.07184

Figure 46 Men in canoes on the Eilanden River, 1936. Photograph taken by A. Pereira. RAI 400.07186

Arthur Pereira explored diagonal compositions in different ways. In **Figure 45** the oars are employed to keep the canoes steady in a strong current whilst in **Figure 46** the diagonally opposed oars at the front of each canoe act as anchors as well as signals to the other men in the boat to cease rowing.

The Eilanden River, one of the longest and widest in the region, proved hospitable. At the river's mouth canoes came out to meet Moyne's party. These meetings involved both the canoeists and Moyne paying close attention to each other.

Both **Figures 47–8** capture this intense concentration of the Asmat matched by Moyne's engagement with them. This is a prelude to undertaking bartering, as had happened previously in both 1929 and 1935. The caption for **Figure 49** written in 1935 by Vera Delves Broughton was clearly designed to underline the exotic and potentially dangerous nature of such encounters. But, peace offerings were quickly made as shown in **Figure 50** from the 1936 trip.

At the same time **Figure 51** shows that the necklaces given by the visitors were being widely worn.

Figure 47 Men in canoes on the Eilanden River, 1936. Photograph taken by A. Pereira. RAI 400.07183

Figure 48 Men in canoes on the Eilanden River, 1936. Photograph taken by A. Pereira. RAI 400.07817

Figure 49 'Walter bartering with the cannibals', Eilanden River, 1935, reproduced in Eastern Cruise 1934/35 album. Photograph taken by Lady Delves Broughton

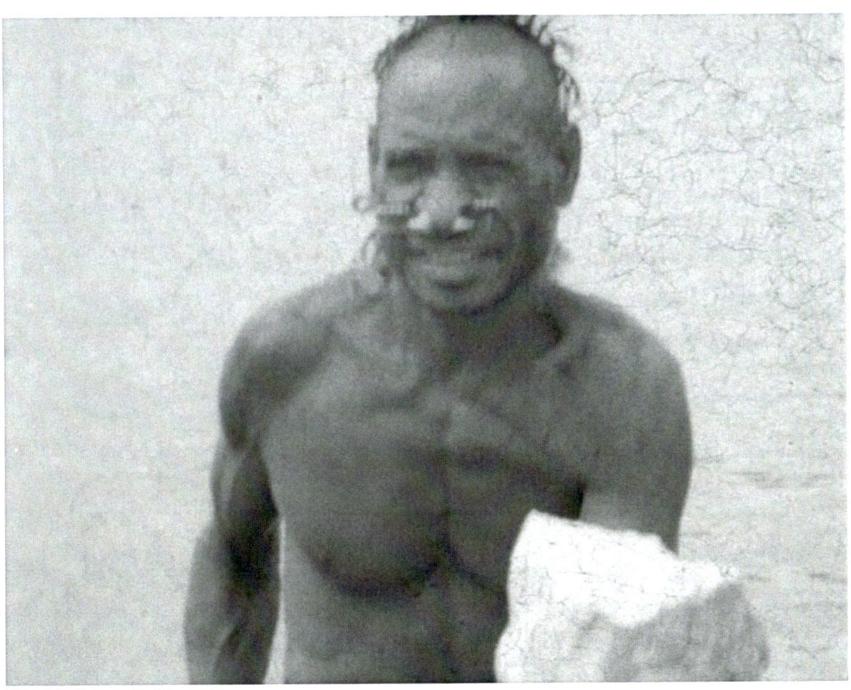

Figure 50 Man offering sago on the Eilanden River, 1936, still from Walkabout film taken by Viscount Elveden

Figure 51 Detail of page from Eastern Trip 1935–36 album, Kampong River, 1936. The photograph shows that the necklaces offered by the visitors were being widely worn. Photograph taken by Lady Delves Broughton

'Lovely girl'

The Eilanden River was also the place where both locals and visitors appeared most relaxed and at ease with each other. This was demonstrated dramatically by the actions of the sole woman in the party, who danced for the visitors. Although Moyne recorded that women and children disappeared whenever he and his party appeared, some women could and did act with curiosity and boldness. Clementine Churchill wrote in her diary for 30 January 1935: 'This morning some of the party went back to get some bows and arrows and were introduced to three Papuan women who jumped on board the launch and didn't seem to want to get off again' (Churchill 1935: 25–6). Again in 1936 two women joined the locals. Moyne wrote: 'One was particularly friendly and seemed to have considerable authority (Moyne 1936a: 44). He called her 'pretty girl' although Delves Broughton's caption (**Fig. 57**) offers a variant, 'Lovely girl'.

Moyne wrote:

> She was delighted with a Woolworth pearl necklace I gave her [**Fig. 52**]. The quick power of imitating sounds which these native possess is very striking. I called one of the ladies 'pretty girl', and she immediately pronounced the words perfectly and went on calling them out to me until we were out of hearing. (Moyne 1936a: 44)

Interestingly, there are no photographs of the second woman, probably because 'she was covered with pink patches from the healing of either burns or some kind of terrible sore' (Moyne 1936a: 44). The epithet 'lovely girl' in this context recognises the vivacity and openness of the first woman towards the visitors.

One of the most engaging sequences in Elveden's Walkabout film is where this woman performs an elaborate dance on a canoe for the benefit of the visitors (**Figs 53–6**).

This is the same person who Moyne had met 13 months previously as can be seen in **Figures 57–8**. Delves Broughton offers a still image of the performance but the 16mm film shows 'lovely girl' also dancing on a canoe as it moves past the visitors' launch on two separate occasions. The two still images reproduced here as **Figures 57–8** are however replete with action.

Whilst the first photograph (**Fig. 57**) demonstrates how close the action is to Moyne, the second image (**Fig. 58**) shows how the dancer recognises the presence of the photographer. The confidence of the dancer is very evident, performing before her audience in their rowing boat rather than on an Asmat canoe. Both the facial expressions and the body gestures of performer and audience member alike attest to their mutual involvement. Dance in Papuan society

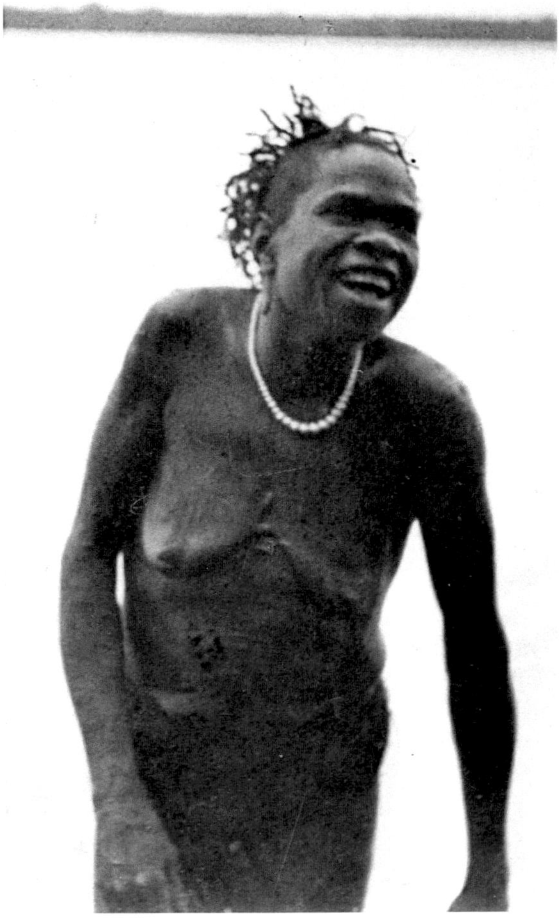

Figure 52 (left) 'Lovely girl in her Woolworths pearls', North Eilanden River, 1936. Photograph taken by Lady Delves Broughton, 1936. RAI 37737

Figure 53 (above) 'Lovely girl' in canoe, 1936, still from Walkabout film taken by Viscount Elveden

has a special role as Boelaars demonstrated when writing about the Jaquai, neighbours of the Asmat. His description of one such dance suggests a setting very similar to the one discussed here. He wrote: 'the arrival of guests always took place towards the evening, the sun shining up the golden shimmer of the swaying birds of paradise on their heads. Some women, the best dancers of the community, stood in their small canoes at a short distance from the bank, twisting and rolling their hips, enthralling the spectators with their balance and graceful motion' (Boelaars 1981: 153). This was the kind of show that Moyne's party enjoyed in 1936.

Paul Carter, writing about theatrical enactment in encounter settings such as these, suggests that 'the intercourse the natives and the newcomers initiate is, potentially at least, imitative, reciprocal and self contained' (Carter 1992: 176). He insists that 'in this situation the space of the performance becomes the means of marking out a common place of utterance, where in the future perhaps, sounds and meanings may settle down and become social bonds' (Carter 2004: 130). Whilst the photographic evidence in this case suggests that something equivalent to a playful relationship was established between the female performer and Moyne, it is perhaps fanciful to extrapolate

Figure 54 'Lovely girl' in canoe, 1936, still from Walkabout film taken by Viscount Elveden

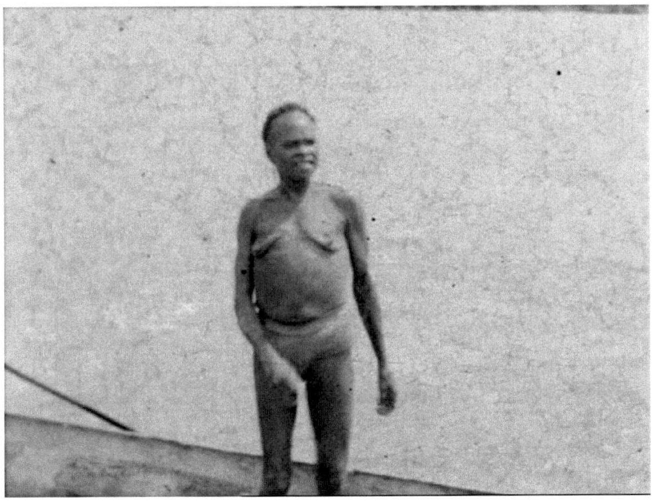

Figure 55 'Lovely girl' dancing, 1936, still from Walkabout film taken by Viscount Elveden

Figure 56 'Lovely girl' dancing in dinghy, 1936, still from Walkabout film taken by Viscount Elveden

Figure 57 '"Lovely girl" dances for Walter', Eilanden River, 1935, reproduced in Eastern Cruise 1934/35 album. Photograph taken by Lady Delves Broughton

Figure 58 '"Lovely girl" dances for Walter', Eilanden River, 1935, reproduced in Eastern Cruise 1934/35 album. Photograph taken by Lady Delves Broughton

from this any kind of lasting deep rapport, even though they had renewed their acquaintance on at least one occasion. There is no suggestion in this case that any members of the visiting party imitated the dancer but the performance was sufficient of itself, in its repetition and re-enactment, to remind everyone of the pleasure that they shared. No such intimacy or shared memory had been recorded by previous explorers.

Chapter 3
Gifts and Exchanges on the Eilanden and Kampong Rivers

The inhabitants of the Eilanden River were prepared to assist the visitors in their exploration of villages and to engage with them on a regular basis, as **Figure 59** shows. Here locals can be seen taking advantage of the opportunity to proffer goods such as mats as the visitors clambered up the muddy banks in front of the house.

However, the most significant of exchanges took place on the river itself, both in terms of performance (and it has to be recognised that Moyne is as much a performer as 'lovely girl') and in the iconic images of the exchange process itself (**Figs 60–4**). Closer personal contact took place in more difficult circumstances on the Kampong River, Moyne's last port of call in Asmat.

Moyne wrote in 1936: 'our most interesting experiences were on the Kampong River near its junction with the South Eilanden' (Moyne 1936a: 34), which must have been somewhere near the contemporary site of the village of Amanamkai, famed for its carving. A few locals came out to engage in trade as their neighbours had previously done on the Eilanden River (**Figs 65–6**).

Figure 59 Lord Moyne and another European man in a rowing boat, approaching a house where they are met by three Asmat men, two with mats, North Eilanden River, 1936. Photograph taken by Lady Delves Broughton. RAI 400.37727

Figure 60 Scene on Eilanden River, 1936, reproduced in Eastern Trip 1935–36 album. Photograph taken by Lady Delves Broughton

Figure 61 Man trading a bowl on the Eilanden River, 1936. Photograph taken by Lady Delves Broughton. RAI 400.39916

Figure 62 Men in canoe on the Eilanden River, 1936, reproduced in Eastern Trip 1935–36 album. Photograph taken by Lady Delves Broughton

Figure 63 Transfer film footage of exchange on the Eilanden River, 1936. Photograph taken by Lady Delves Broughton

Figure 64 Transfer film footage of exchange on the Eilanden River, 1936. Photograph taken by Lady Delves Broughton

Figure 65 Man in canoe on Eilanden River, 1936, still from Walkabout film taken by Viscount Elveden

Figure 66 'Kampong River Native', 1936, reproduced as Plate 13 in *Walkabout* (Moyne 1936a). Photograph taken by Lady Delves Broughton. British Museum, Oc,B94.44

But, despite Moyne's invitation to begin serious trading, the villagers refused to venture out onto the river. Moyne recorded:

> On our former visits to this region I had noticed that the natives waved mats as an invitation to open friendly relations. For the remaining two hours of day light we repeated this signal and also shouted a native rendering of the name of Roche's launch, as it used to be his habit thus to annouce his arrival and his wish to buy plumage. Although we heard some shouts in answer, no native showed themselves.
> (Moyne 1936a: 35)

The Asmat kept the visitors under surveillance throughout the night, keeping camp fires burning, and the next morning 20 men appeared on the river bank. As the caption in the 1936 album shows (**Fig. 67**), their demeanour was difficult for the visitors to interpret.

It soon became clear that the hosts had come to trade. The sequence and number of photographs taken by Delves Broughton and Pereira demonstrate the importance of the occasion and in particular the mechanics and implicit logic involved in making contact. Whilst it is undoubtedly true

Figure 67 '"Friendly or unfriendly?" Natives of the Kampong River. Note the 15-foot paddle-spear', reproduced as Plate 10 in *Walkabout* (Moyne 1936a). Photograph taken by Lady Delves Broughton. RAI Eastern Trip

Figure 68 Page from Eastern Trip 1935–36 album showing images on the Kampong River, 1936. Photographs taken by Lady Delves Broughton

that the goods that the visitors proffered were, at best, trinkets of little use-value to them, such as cheap imitation pearl necklaces and empty bottles, these objects were nevertheless fascinating novelties to their recipients, and they were ones that they clearly wanted. The tension surrounding this meeting was noted by Moyne:

> We saw several canoes lurking in the backwater, but the natives would not respond to our signals to come out to the launches which were anchored just out of bow-shot from the entrance to the creek. We therefore went in on the dinghies. Vera and I opened up trading for the native weapons and the now prohibited birds of paradise feathers in exchange for knives, empty bottles etc., while Arthur and Rosamond in the other dinghy lay off with firearms to cover us from sudden attack. There was so much suspicion on both sides that the natives were very unwilling to come alongside us in their canoes and we realised that it would be unwise to risk landing and encirclement by a well-armed crowd. The trading therefore had to be done from a dinghy with the natives who came into the shallow river margin to meet us.
> (Moyne 1936a: 36)

The visitors were evidently impressed by what was displayed on the river bank and the scene was captured on the album page reproduced here as **Figure 68**. The tension was broken as soon as the Asmat men stepped into the river as a subsequent album page shows (**Fig. 69**).

At once, the invitation to the visitors was clear. The four images move successively from the top left with the two Asmat men stepping into the river to the man in the top right

Figure 69 Page from Eastern Trip 1935–36 album showing images on the Kampong River, 1936, with the caption 'Kampong native offering to trade his weapons'. Photographs taken by Lady Delves Broughton

photograph engaging the visitors through the offer of bows and arrows. The bottom left photograph was taken shortly after its predecessor with the bow already offered. The last of the four images appears to have been taken after the bow and arrows were traded as the Kampong man then went on to offer a bird-of-paradise plume. What happened next seems to contradict Moyne's account cited above in one significant respect. The next sequence of images does not show Moyne and Delves Broughton in one dinghy and Rosamond and Elveden in the other. As the first picture (**Fig. 70**) shows, Moyne is rowing a dinghy to the river bank with Rosamond in the stern, two bottles at her side which would later be used in exchange, whilst the Kampong trader presents a spear as his companions on the river bank hold spears and a paddle.

The second image (**Fig. 71**) shows closer engagement and the third of this tripych (**Fig. 72**) captures the moment of exchange. When this last image (**Fig. 72**) is enlarged it becomes apparent that what Rosamond is holding is a bunch of carpenter's nails which she is counting out as payment for the plume.

Elveden's Walkabout film shows Rosamond stepping from the dinghy onto the river bank beside the men from the Kampong whilst her mother is taking a photograph of the event and Moyne is keeping the boat steady with his oars (**Fig. 73**). Out in the river Moyne was probably well aware of the danger faced by both parties in the immediate moment and this is evident in this set of images. Unlike his fellow soldiers Meyjes and de Rochemont (see **Figs 7–8**) two decades earlier, he was also an adventurer and quite

Figure 70 Lord Moyne, Rosamond Delves Broughton and local trader, Kampong River, 1936. Photograph taken by Lady Delves Broughton. RAI 400.37735

Figure 71 Rosamond Delves Broughton trading from boat, Kampong River, 1936. Photograph taken by Lady Delves Broughton. RAI 400.37739

Figure 72 Rosamond Delves Broughton trading nails for a plume with a native, Kampong River, 1936. Photograph taken by Lady Delves Broughton. RAI 37736

Figure 73 Rosamond Delves Broughton stepping from the dinghy onto the river bank, Kampong River, 1936, still from Walkabout film taken by Viscount Elveden

prepared to take risks. The photographs here record his willingness to engage in the process of trade and exchange.

One question that this series of images raises is why Rosamond played such a prominent role in the exchange process. As Moyne's text made plain, the event was fraught with potential difficulty for both parties and both courage and determination were in constant need. Perhaps Rosamond's vulnerability was an asset. There are no photographs in any of the collections of Rosamond holding a gun, though the Walkabout film does show her mother stepping ashore with a rifle in hand on the Eilanden, covering Moyne as he approaches a men's house. Like 'lovely girl' on the Eilanden, Rosamond took significant risks in the close encounters on the banks of the Kampong River and placed considerable trust in her trading partners.

Things did not always work out so well. At the next village Moyne recorded the following incident:

> We were not able to do any trading here, although a few men finally showed themselves. One had a beautiful paradise plume. He was afraid, however, to come down to where Vera was holding onto a tree under the steep bank. He therefore began to tie it onto a very sharp spear so as to throw it to her in the dinghy in exchange for a knife which she held up for him to see. While she was signalling to him not to throw the spear, Arthur, who was covering us with a gun near-by in the other boat, called out to us to be careful as there was a man preparing to shoot an arrow. On turning round I saw a person of very unfriendly appearance crouched behind a log and fitting an arrow to his bow-string. I therefore quickly sculled out into the stream. Whether from fear or guilty conscience the natives then ran away and although we lay near-by for the night and landed to examine their huts we were quite unable to entice them back. (Moyne 1936a: 38–9)

Moyne concluded that the inhabitants of the rivers lived under conditions of constant insecurity and that all strangers were considered enemies. But this was not always the case, as shown in the previous chapter.

Moyne's last successful trading was with his 'friends we made on a previous visit' near the mouth of the Eilanden River, who may have had some regular experience of trade. Here, he observed that: 'the natives were quite friendly and willing to trade well-carved sago bowls and flutes made of bamboo, partly closed at one end by a perforated node'. Moyne reflected on the process of trading: 'They showed their ignorance of European products by the equal eagerness with which they accepted knives, a few nails, empty bottles or petrol tins, in exchange for the weapons or utensils' (Moyne 1936a: 41). This was in contrast to the Kampong River where there was a ready appreciation for iron goods such as bush knives and hatchets. He put this lack of discrimination down to the Kampong River inhabitants' unfamiliarity with foreign traders such as Roche, but this explanation seems hardly adequate to account for the disparity of behaviour. A fuller explanation has to take into account the activites and sensitivities of both parties.

What the photographic record demonstrates is the degree of trust and enjoyment that both hosts and visitors experienced in their mutual encounter. Neither party, of course, let down their defences or trusted each other fully as they bartered. There is in each photograph a keen tension, a feeling that contact might be broken off at any moment. The surprise is that, under these circumstances, this did not happen and that contact was sustained over several visits. This was something that had not happened in previously recorded encounters between Asmat and other visitors. Nor was it to recur until well into the period of missionisation in the 1950s.

Chapter 4
Creating the Record

Making the collection

Although Moyne was keen to have first-hand experience of the places that he visited in the Pacific, he always kept in mind his other objective of making artefact collections for the British Museum. He was especially eager to make acquisitions in Papua, partly because the area was not well represented in the British Museum, but also, as he explained:

> It was especially in Netherlands New Guinea and on the Ramu River that we were able to find products of native craftsmanship in their pure state, before the modification of primitive traditions by culture contact or race mixture. Especially in Netherlands New Guinea on the Bloemen, Eilanden and Kampong rivers we were able to find carved woodwork showing the origin of pattern from human and animal forms. The original crude representation of the human body here persists side by side with innumerable variations derived from it, but so metamorphosed that their origin could only be traced by careful examination. The instinctive symmetry of design is very striking and in curious contrast to some of the ultra-modern schools which profess to hold native models in such high esteem. We found the best wood decoration where it had been carried out with the most primitive instruments, where metal tools were unknown and the work had been done with shell and bone and red-hot wood. This primitive art will quickly disappear from the world, for it seems capable of offering no resistance to competition with imported forms. When the missionary or recruiter of labour arrives with his trade goods, the indigenous models at once become modified by civilised examples and tools of steel.
> (Moyne 1936a: 283–4)

Moyne's preference for 'primitive art' perhaps reflects the tuition that he had received from Braunholtz at the British Museum. On his return from his first visit to Asmat in 1929, Moyne's donation to the Museum contained ten shields from the Eilanden and Kampong rivers which Braunholtz studied carefully. In 1934 Braunholtz published his design theory in *The British Museum Quarterly*:

> The designs, carved all over the frontal surface, are outlined by pairs and narrow and more or less parallel ridges, enclosing broad grooves or channels, which are invariably painted red, the remainder of the sunk background being whitened with lime, and certain details added in black. A bold and distinctive effect, suggestive of cloisonné work, is produced by this 'ridge-and-groove' style. All principal designs appear to be derived from the human form, and, when arranged in a series, illustrates in an admirable way the principle of degeneration from zoomorphic to geometric forms.
> (Braunholtz 1934: 153–4)

Braunholtz selected three shields to demonstrate his thesis concerning the development of abstraction in the human form in his figs 1–3 reproduced here in **Figure 74**.

Moyne commented: 'A series of shields which I brought home on a previous visit was worked out by Mr. H.J. Braunholtz to show how designs found on the human form develop into a geometrical pattern of which the original elements would hardly be suspected unless they could be traced back through a whole series' (Moyne 1936a: 44).

Moyne's comparison between primitive art and its modern counterpart (and here he was probably thinking more of cubism than surrealism) favoured the former

Figure 74 'Carved and painted wood shields from Dutch New Guinea' (Braunholtz 1934: 152). Fig. 1 (left) is British Museum, Oc1934,0316.7; Fig. 2 (centre) is British Museum, Oc1934,0316.4; Fig. 3 (right) is British Museum, Oc1934,0316.2

Figure 76 Inside the *je*, Momogu, 2008. Photograph taken by the author

Figure 75 Display of shields at Asmat Museum of Culture and Progress, Agats, mounted in 1995 and photographed by the author in 2011

because of its adherence to geometric symmetry. However, Moyne's prognosis for the future of Asmat art was full of gloom. He believed that missionaries and traders would defeat the purity of design, driving it out with trade goods and destroying its strength with the introduction of steel chisels. Moyne would therefore have been very surprised to see a display of contemporary shields as exhibited in 1995 in the Asmat Museum of Culture and Progress (**Fig. 75**) or the ubiquity of shields in the villages (**Fig. 76**).

The other large items that Moyne collected, especially the house posts on the Bloemen River, are still made. The post collected in 1936 (**Fig. 77**) is notably similar to those currently found in *je* (men's houses) throughout Asmat (**Figs 78–9**).

With an eye for design, Moyne also collected dance items including horns (*fu*). He noted: 'we visited three villages within fifteen miles of the mouth of the Northern Eilanden ... the natives were quite friendly and willing to trade well-carved sago bowls and flutes made of bamboo, partly closed at one end by a perforated node' (Moyne 1936a: 41). Contemporary horns have the same design features as those collected by Moyne (see **Figs 80–2**). Alongside horns Moyne also obtained drums, an essential instrument used to accompany dances (**Fig. 83**).

He recorded whilst in a village on the Bloemen River: 'We also found ten drums and various axe shaped instruments for beating sago' (Moyne 1936a: 28). Such drums are still in use today (**Fig. 84**).

Perhaps one of the most iconic objects to figure so prominently in the visual record is the crocodile jaw bone dagger that features in Plate 11 of *Walkabout* (**Figs 16–17, 85**). This object evidently intrigued Moyne as he wrote:

> [On the South Eilanden River] About twenty natives eventually came down to each side of the creek opening, some armed with bows and arrows and spears whilst others carried very businesslike daggers made of cassowary bone or from half the jaw of a crocodile. The crocodile daggers were particularly

Figure 77 House post collected by Lord Moyne in 1936. British Museum, Oc1936,0720.243

Figure 78 House post *in situ* in *je*, Bu-Agani, 2011. Photograph taken by the author

Figure 79 Modern day house posts, *je*, Sjuru, 2005. Photograph taken by the author

Figure 80 *Fu* (horn) made of bamboo, collected by Lord Moyne in 1936. British Museum, Oc1936,0720.233

Figure 81 (above) Modern *fu* made of bamboo, from Sjuru, 2011. Author's collection

Figure 82 (left) Detail of horn in Fig. 81

Figure 83 *Em* (drum) made of wood and rattan, collected by Lord Moyne in 1936. British Museum, Oc1936,0720.236

Figure 84 Dance festival in Agats 2011. Photograph taken by the author

> effective, some being two feet long. The ends of bone towards the reptile's head are tapered from a broad cutting edge to a very sharp point, while the front corner tooth of the crocodile is invariably retained at the top either to improve the grip or perhaps to be used as a pole-axe in case of need.
> (Moyne 1936a: 35–6)

Moyne's collection represents a compendium of Asmat design found on all the carved wooden objects that he had selected. There are however a range of carvings that did not come his way, principally *wuramon* (souls ships) that take the form of men and birds sitting in a canoe without a bottom. Neither was he offered perhaps the most well-known kind of carving from Asmat, the *bisj* or ancestor pole. These huge carvings of a series of ancestor figures piled one on top of another with a *cemen* or phallus extension reach as high as four to five metres. Such poles can be seen most dramatically in the Michael Rockefeller display in Gallery 354 in the Metropolitan Museum of Art, New York (**Fig. 86**).

Why, when he was in the region of their manufacture, did Moyne fail to obtain such dramatic achievements of Asmat

Figure 85 Photograph of the bone dagger made from crocodile jaw bone (British Museum, Oc1936,0720.229) collected by Lord Moyne in 1936 (as seen in Figs 16–17). British Museum, Oc,B23.6

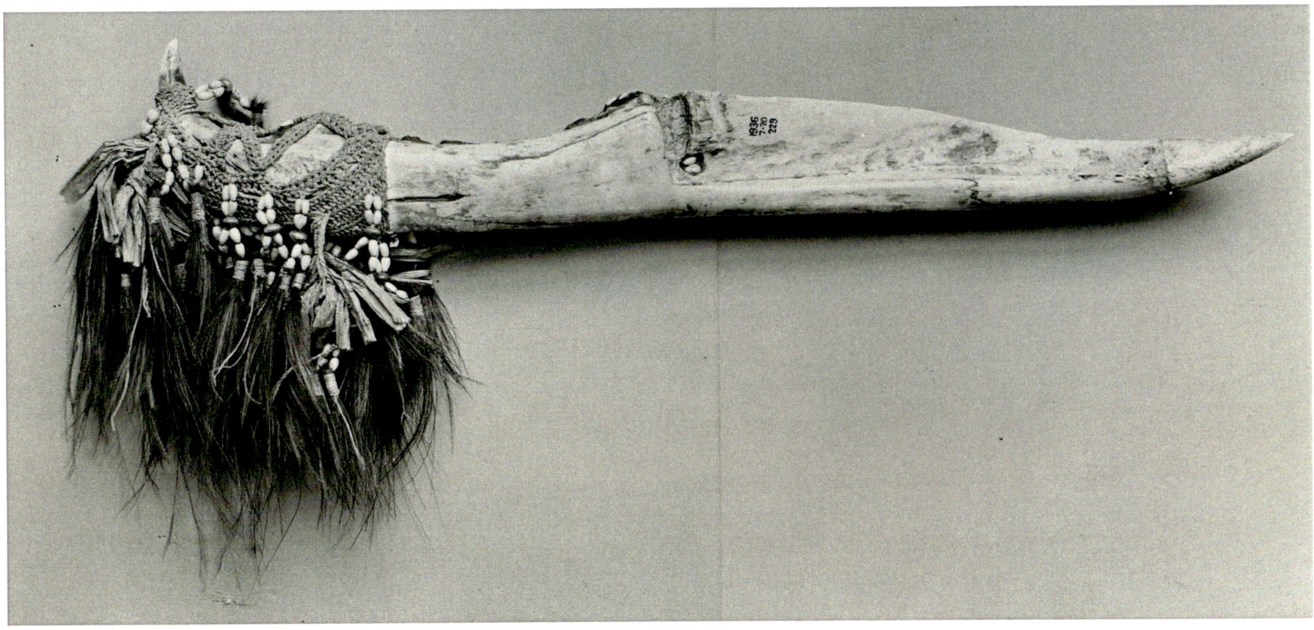

Figure 86 *Bisj* poles from Omadesep in Gallery 354, Metropolitan Museum of Art, New York, 2009. Photograph taken by the author

Figure 87 'At Merauke, the Capital', photograph taken by Lord Moyne in 1929 and reproduced in 'Travels WEG' album

Figure 88 Work for sale at the annual carving contest, Agats, 2005. Photograph taken by the author

carving? The answer is probably very straightforward. They were not portable, and as Moyne did not have sufficient time to explore the territory fully, he would not have been aware of their existence. Without his prompting it would probably not have occurred to the carvers that these were valuable assets to bargain with.

Moyne was certain that he was preserving for posterity evidence of an artistic culture that was doomed to perish. The contemporary examples shown in this chapter testify to the inaccuracy of Moyne's prognosis. Why was he so wrong? It would seem that his views were based on visual evidence from his first visit to Merauke to the east of the Asmat district in 1929 when he came in contact with the Marind Anim as shown in **Figure 87**.

The Marind Anim were a clothed people who had already ceased to live in traditional ways and had been moved into colonial settlements. Crucially, they had also stopped making their *angei-aha* (ceremonial houses) or constructing their ritual towers. The Marind Anim were, in the words of a missionary, 'now broken and robbed of his land' (Corbey 2010: 26). They were not alone. Other peoples along the south coast of Papua went into a similar artistic decline. It was therefore logical that Moyne would project such a future onto the Asmat people. The earlier question can now be rephrased: how did the Asmat escape this fate and remain active and innovative carvers? The short answer is that they found a way to bring the activity and the aesthetic design vocabulary into the modern world of commodity production. Through good fortune, both the missionaries and the early traders who did eventually arrive saw the potential for the sale of this remarkable work, created a local museum to display it in, set up a United Nations Development Project to promote its production and sale, and founded an annual carving festival to showcase contemporary work which thrives today (**Fig. 88**).

Moyne's fascination with material culture has resulted in an excellent visual source of reference in the history of Asmat carving. What is abundantly clear is that the designs he observed on shields, drums and horns still persist today with remarkable fidelity. The vocabulary of Asmat design remains instantly recognisable and distinct. This distinctive quality was one of the characteristics that drew Moyne back time and again to visit the region and to acquire 'very good carving' which gives 'a very bold and pleasing effect' (Moyne 1936a: 44).

Holding an exhibition

What could be more satisfying than bringing the results of the voyage together in one place? Moyne held an exhibition of 300 artefacts collected during his voyage in 1935/6 and showed them together with Delves Broughton's contextual photographs and Arthur Elveden's 16mm film in the ballroom of his town house in London. H.J. Braunholtz provided substantial support. Firstly he was involved in writing the exhibition catalogue as he noted in a letter to A.C. Haddon on 19 May 1936: 'We have just finished the

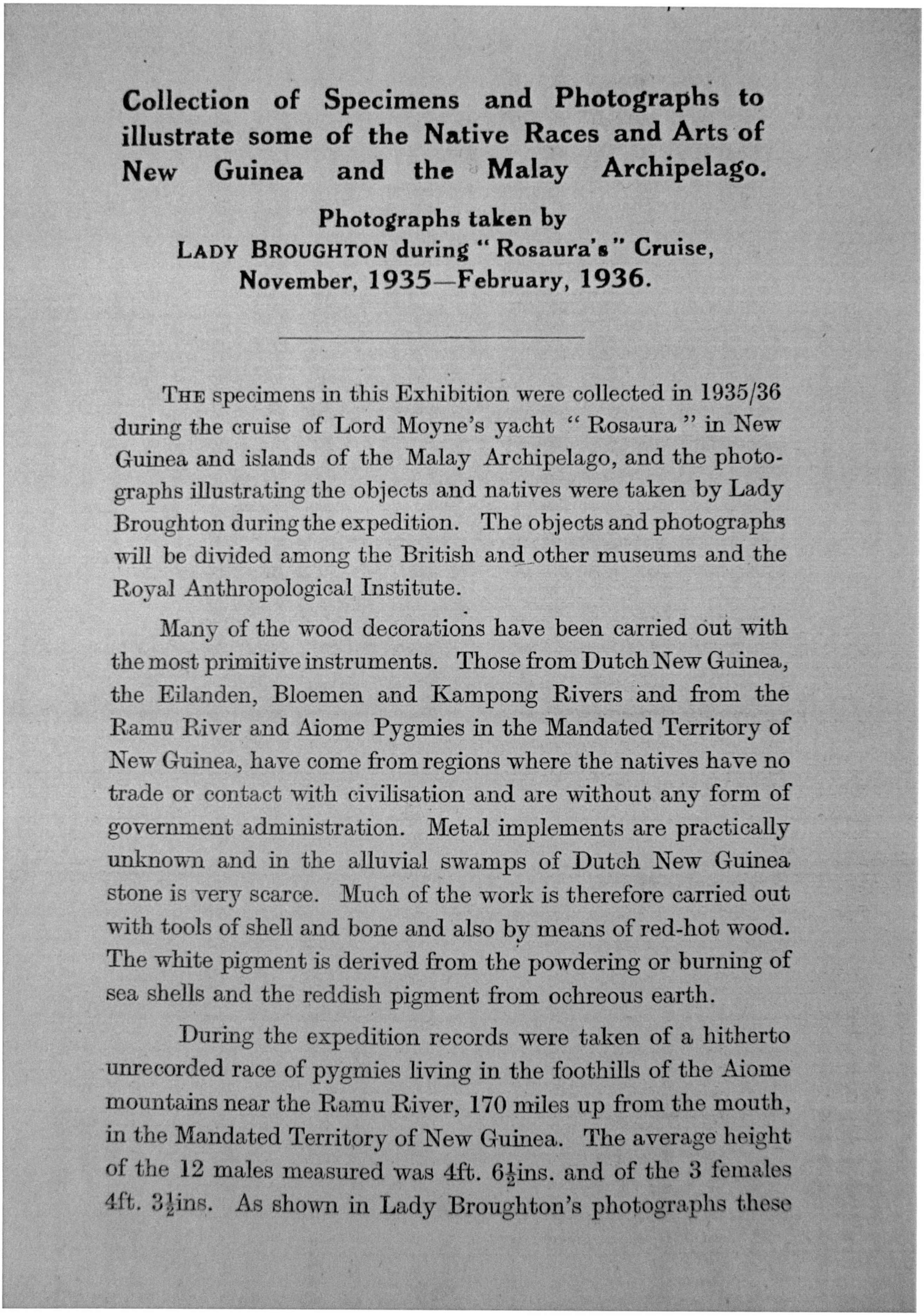

Collection of Specimens and Photographs to illustrate some of the Native Races and Arts of New Guinea and the Malay Archipelago.

Photographs taken by
LADY BROUGHTON during " Rosaura's " Cruise,
November, 1935—February, 1936.

THE specimens in this Exhibition were collected in 1935/36 during the cruise of Lord Moyne's yacht " Rosaura " in New Guinea and islands of the Malay Archipelago, and the photographs illustrating the objects and natives were taken by Lady Broughton during the expedition. The objects and photographs will be divided among the British and other museums and the Royal Anthropological Institute.

Many of the wood decorations have been carried out with the most primitive instruments. Those from Dutch New Guinea, the Eilanden, Bloemen and Kampong Rivers and from the Ramu River and Aiome Pygmies in the Mandated Territory of New Guinea, have come from regions where the natives have no trade or contact with civilisation and are without any form of government administration. Metal implements are practically unknown and in the alluvial swamps of Dutch New Guinea stone is very scarce. Much of the work is therefore carried out with tools of shell and bone and also by means of red-hot wood. The white pigment is derived from the powdering or burning of sea shells and the reddish pigment from ochreous earth.

During the expedition records were taken of a hitherto unrecorded race of pygmies living in the foothills of the Aiome mountains near the Ramu River, 170 miles up from the mouth, in the Mandated Territory of New Guinea. The average height of the 12 males measured was 4ft. 6½ins. and of the 3 females 4ft. 3½ins. As shown in Lady Broughton's photographs these

Figure 89 Front page of the catalogue accompanying the Walkabout exhibition of 1936. British Museum, Eth.Doc 1004

Figure 90 'Dazzling the Enemy: Shields from the Pacific' exhibition, British Museum, 2009

brief catalogue of the Moyne exhibition, and it has gone to press' (**Fig. 89**).

Braunholtz was keen to publicise the exhibition and inserted a two-page review of the material displayed in the June 1936 edition of *Man*. The notice began: 'By the kind courtesy of Lord Moyne an exhibition of the large and varied collection of ethnographical specimens formed by him on his recent expedition (1935–6) to New Guinea and Indonesia will be opened to the public from Tuesday 26th May for several weeks at 10 Grosvenor Place, S.W. 1 from 11. a.m. to 6 p.m.' The flyer for the exhibition added: 'A small entrance fee will be charged, and the proceeds will be utilized in the interests of anthropology.' The catalogue was more specific: 'The proceeds of the exhibition will be given to the Royal Anthropological Institute, whose monthly journal "Man," contains several photographs of the exhibition, is on sale.' A close inspection of **Figure 26** shows the objects numbered (with cloakroom tickets) in precisely the order in which they appeared in the catalogue. What is immediately apparent when inspecting the catalogue is the geographic specificity of the display. Only the island of New Guinea and its outlying New Britain and the Trobriand Islands receive full attention. There are a few objects from Borneo and the Nicobar Islands, but the overwhelming majority of the items come from the Bloemen, Kampong and Eilanden rivers in South Papua and from the Ramu River and the Sepik River on the north coast.

The catalogue was mainly a listing of items with their provenance given in a few terse words. There are occasional academic references, nearly all to Braunholtz's publications. There is only one small flash of excitement at the end of the exhibition, and, as might be expected, it relates to Asmat. Item 298 reads:

> Collection of Cassowary and human bones found hanging in a house in a deserted village on the Eilanden River. The human bones were of two left scapulae and two lower jaws. They were in a moderately fresh condition when found, with some flesh adhering. The fact that they were tied up over the hearth with various bones of cassowary makes it improbable that they were mementoes of friends and relations and points to the likelihood of the collection being used for the purpose of food.

The exhibition ended in June, as Braunholtz reported (Braunholtz 1937: 164). It was not a great success as Moyne admitted to Henry Balfour: 'I am sending you copies of our catalogue. We have plenty to spare as not many of the public came to the exhibition' (Moyne 1936d). Why was the exhibition not more popular? The press articles of the 1935 trip written by Moyne and Delves Broughton and accompanied by Delves Broughton's photographs were widely read. Maybe a year later the topic was no longer of such interest? But perhaps the venue bears the main responsibility. It was neither a recognised museum nor an art gallery. Nevertheless it attracted specialist interest as D.J. Kunst of the Royal Colonial Institute, Amsterdam, shows in his photographs (see **Fig. 26**).

What was the fate of the collected objects once they had been distributed to the three museums? A shield, a paddle and a throwing spear are still on display in the Upper Gallery at the Pitt Rivers Museum as well as masks and a squatting ancestor figure in the Lower Gallery (Miley 2008: 1). Louis Clarke at Cambridge regretted that the bulk of Moyne's collection had gone to the British Museum and commented: 'I know he has given his ethnographical collection to the British Museum where, alas! they are confined to the basement' (Clarke 1936a). He aimed to do better with the small collection that went to Cambridge. He wrote a memo to his staff: 'Please consider the idea of hanging some New Guinea shields on the back of the case containing the Eskimo things' (Clarke 1936b). Clarke's forecast for the future of Moyne's donation to the British Museum, to be left languishing in the basement, has not proven entirely accurate. Three shields and Delves Broughton's 'Man offering shield, Eilanden River' (**Fig. 6**) were displayed in the 2009 exhibition 'Dazzling the Enemy: Shields from the Pacific' (**Fig. 90**).

Chapter 5
Conclusions

What do these photographs tell us about Asmat and how important are they? They provide a vivid set of images of a people in a pre-colonial setting at a very late stage in Western imperial expansion. The photographs provide an introduction to the history of Asmat, showing aspects of life that contrast with later imagery when the Indonesian state sought a more 'modern' vision which they promoted through the officially sponsored Asmat Foundation (Yayasan Kemajuan dan Pengembanan Asmat: YKPA) (**Fig. 91**). The Foundation blamed Western tourists and antique dealers for the alleged decline in standards of craftmanship over the years, but did little in effect to modernise production (Stanley 2012: 156).

The Walkabout photographs also complement Moyne's text, though occasionally they question the written narrative as has been highlighted in the previous chapters. They also offer the reader some pause for reflection concerning the ethical decisions made (or not made) by Moyne's party, especially when the local inhabitants were not consulted or recompensed for the removal of such culturally significant items as skulls and ceremonial house posts. The photographs help situate the 293 artefacts donated to the British Museum, the 141 to the Pitt Rivers Museum and the 8 to the Cambridge University Museum of Archaeology and Anthropology, showing how canoes and paddles worked, and how objects of personal adornment such as the *bipane* (nose plug) were worn. The photographs also give us an understanding of the architecture of the *je* (men's house), which still looks remarkably similar today. Perhaps as importantly, they also offer an intimate picture of the visitors and their interaction with a variety of local people. In addition, they document the extraordinary way in which the adventure was possible thanks to the financial resources which supported the *Rosaura* with its up-to-the-minute technology (for example echo-sounding equipment), motor launches and skilled personnel including photographers such as Vera Delves Broughton and Arthur Pereira, as well as the cine-camera operated by Arthur Elveden.

Figure 91 Opening of the YKPA Pusan Asmat (Asmat Centre), April 1989. Photographer unknown

Figures 92–4 Cutting down the effigy figure from the long house, Bloemen River, 1936, stills from Walkabout film taken by Viscount Elveden

What does this photographic survey accomplish and how does it stand the test of time? In the photographic record there is no visual equivalence of Moyne's objective of salvage ethnography that is so prominently expressed in his text. The only photographs that dwell on decay and poverty are those that show the mouldering empty huts on the Bloemen River, but these are devoid of people. Whilst Delves Broughton's Asmat imagery does commemorate the persistence of the archaic in the modern world, it does not constitute a proper narrative. It cannot be an ethnographic study without an accompanying verbal account. All that could be captured was the moment. In the end that is what we are bequeathed: a series of vignettes partially illuminated by Moyne's text and Delves Broughton's captions. What the construction of the albums also provided was a grouping, sequencing and intense inspection of the events and scenarios brought together on a single page. We can infer quite a lot about the values of the photographers and editors from these photographs and their captions – Delves Broughton in her albums and Moyne in *Walkabout*. A sense of adventure permeates the work. As the images show, each setting produced fresh opportunities and new challenges, whether in the silent villages of the Bloemen River, meetings in the expanse of the Eilanden River estuary or in close encounters on the banks of the Kampong River. In each case the photographs also graphically document the process of acquisition through collecting and exchange. For example, the photographs record the enthusiastic acquisition by the visitors and equally enthusiastic exchange by the villagers of iconic objects such as shields (see for example **Figs 6** and **22**). In extreme cases, the cine-camera recorded violent acquisition such as the incident on the Bloemen River when Moyne chopped a ceremonial post off from the house that it was decorating or protecting (**Figs 92–4**).

This sequence shows the visitors engaged in the act of acquisition, and raises for us doubts about the ethical propriety of some of their actions. If the film sequence tells us very little from 'the native point of view', it helps us understand the visitors' actions. The imagery also contradicts Moyne's narrative at key junctures, such as the role of Rosamond Delves Broughton (**Fig. 95**), which does not appear in the text of *Walkabout*. With the film footage, the photographers also give detailed examples of rowing and navigation on the network of rivers to amplify the written record.

To what contemporary use can this imagery be put? How can the record contribute to Asmat today? Initially, these questions are not easy to answer. There is in the world of museums a growing tradition of offering cultural restitution of past acquisitions that were based on inequitable exchanges. But in reality, in places like South Papua, it is difficult to engage in cultural restitution of any kind because of the complications and entanglement involved in the original intercourse between uninvited European explorers and their often reluctant hosts. Nowhere is this more explicit than in the case of the Walkabout photographic records.

Figure 95 Rosamond Delves Broughton taking possession of the crocodile dagger on the Kampong River, 1936, still from Walkabout film taken by Viscount Elveden

Figure 96 David Jiminipitsj from Ewer consulting *Walkabout* (Moyne 1936a), Agats, 2010. Photograph taken by the author

The political changes in Papua since Indonesian rule further complicate the situation as I explain later.

One of the most important and vexatious problems occurs when the original setting for the encounter is one where a European understanding of history is not employed. So, for example, taking these 70-year-old photographs back to Asmat and showing them to contemporary Asmat elders or youngsters does not immediately engender either recognition or rapport (**Fig. 96**). The cultural and generational distance is too large for this to occur spontaneously. There is also a major question of to whom these photographs should be returned. My very unsatisfactory solution to the conundrum is perhaps not that different to the one used by Lord Moyne in the deserted villages. I have deposited copies of both still photographs and the 16mm film with the Asmat Museum of Culture and Progress. Of course the next question is what will the museum do with the images? Currently the answer is unclear because there is little cultural infrastructure in place to work with this imagery. What is missing is a methodology of reconnection to a previous past: bringing the past history into the new circumstances of education and cultural revival (Newbury 2015: 65). But I remain hopeful that this visual cultural record can become an efficient heritage resource for the future. I am encouraged by Azoulay's statement that the reading of a photograph is not fixed by the author: 'it will always turn out that something else can be read in it, some other event can be reconstructed from it, some other player's presence can be discerned through it' (Azoulay 2008: 12).

Azoulay also reminds us that photographs have a life independent of the event that gave rise to their creation (Azoulay 2012: 26). We do not need to be burdened with the intentions of the photographer to appreciate or employ the imagery. 'Lovely girl', for example, in her various appearances offers her own perspective on the meetings captured on camera by Delves Broughton. In one particular respect the photographs can act as a major resource. They show people interacting in their local environment and with everyday objects. In certain cases they provide evidence of what is no longer in circulation. Canoe construction is currently a dying art: there are no longer trees tall enough to construct war canoes, but we can examine these historic images for vital evidence to help in attempts to revive the art of canoe manufacture.

The many ways of reading images saves the Asmat photographs taken by Moyne, Delves Broughton, Elveden and Periera from being restricted to an imperial imagination with its cultural assumptions of evolutionary determinism, or to tropes of commercial exploitation. It also helps that Moyne, although very much influenced by beliefs that we may now find uncomfortable such as the typification of human peoples by racial types, writes about and shows pictures of the Asmat as people with very special skills and aptitudes. River craft and sculptural prowess impressed him greatly. His collections, made for museums, were carefully selected to illustrate a specific Asmat aesthetic whilst the photographs and films demonstrated the mechanics of cultural encounter as well as the way in which the Asmat mastered their particular world.

One of the major projects to which Moyne and his party can now contribute is the creation of an historic record of the Asmat people and the continuities within its cultural development. This is vitally important. If the Dutch colonial regime until 1963 can be best characterised as one of benevolent neglect, the Indonesian administration since then has been very active in Papua. From the beginning of the new regime the lack of clothing of the inhabitants of West Papua was seen by their new rulers as both offensive and a cause for national shame. They became merely 'stone age' people. In 1969, the year in which Papua was finally incorporated into Indonesia, President Suharto reflected on a set of photographs of scantily clad Papuans taken soon after the implementation of the 'Act of Free Choice' that ushered in the new regime. He commented: 'I'm sure, however: dead material as they may be, these photographs will nevertheless speak straight to the heart of everyone who looks at them. If we accept these photos and look at them with our conscience, see them with our hearts and mind, we cannot possibly remain unconcerned' (Suharto 1969: 8). The image of unclothed Papuans demanded immediate action to make them 'fully human' (*haruslа kita mejadikan mereka manusia*). To encourage people to become 'modern' and wear shorts and shirts the government introduced a policy entitled Operasi Koteka (Operation Penis Sheath) in 1971. At the same time the administration in Asmat proscribed feasting and meeting in men's houses, and to ensure compliance burned the buildings down every time they were erected. This policy continued uninterrupted from 1964 to 1971 (Sowada 2002: 53). From this point onwards historic photographs could only signify primitiveness and so were emblems of all that was offensive. To change the situation even more radically the Indonesian government introduced a policy entitled *transmigrasi* (transmigration) that encouraged people from the western part of Indonesia, especially Java, to settle in the area. The policy has been so successful that Papuans now represent less than half the population of the region. Consequently the record of previous ages becomes successively more attenuated. For these reasons the few historic visual records that survive take on an additional significance.

One of the most obvious features of the Walkabout imagery of the Asmat is the uninhibited and ever-present male naked form. Apart from a few cases of ringworm suffered by some of the men, there is no picture of other diseases or deformities such as 'elephantiasis and horrible sores' that Moyne mentions in his text (Moyne 1936a: 41). These are emphatically heroic figures that defy the Indonesian concept of decorum through dress. Moyne ventured into Asmat, 'beyond the regions of semi-civilized natives dressed in cheap pyjamas and badly fitting European clothes and to find human and animal life in primitive conditions' (Moyne 1935: 17). He was explicit in his disapproval of importing clothes. He read a Dutch Government publication on 'Protecting the primitive natives' and underlined the following text with approval:

> Clothing presumes a certain degree of civilization. Free importation of clothes, ready made ones especially, leads to a hunt for them from no other grounds than vanity. The moral effect therefore is utterly problematic. The effect on health is of a decidedly negative nature, as long as there is no guidance. Such clothes namely [*sic*] are never washed and soon hang around the body of the wearer as sticky rags. Cutaneous diseases are thus benefitted, but it is more serious that all sorts of infectious matters find a propitious soil to flourish in. (Netherlands Committee for International Nature Protection 1938: 22)

Perhaps it was because of this disdain for shoddy clothing that Moyne did not take bolts of cloth along to barter with, unlike most subsequent visitors to Papua. Whilst Moyne's language played into the later Indonesian concept of the 'primitive', he was in fact attempting to warn of some of the unintended consequences of government and missionary schemes to make people modern by clothing them. The Walkabout imagery refuses to regard modernisation as a taken-for-granted good, emphasising instead the persistence of admirable characteristics associated with pre-modern life. There is, nevertheless, an open question as to how contemporary Asmat individuals now regard this imagery. The fact that nearly everyone in Asmat now wears shorts perhaps suggests that the Indonesian agenda has been accomplished. However, during contemporary feasts today the issue of nakedness is still live. Joshua Irwandi, a documentary photographer, recently wrote the following to me:

> I was photographing a Jipae feast in Jeni. Some of the people weren't too pleased to see me there. One requested me not to turn the photographs into CD-ROMs: '*Kita ini sudah telanjang!*' exclaimed one – 'we are all naked now!' When he said that I guess it's about the fact that Asmat feasts have been publicised more than they wanted (especially Jipae feasts where masks of their ancestors' likenesses are out) and they get nothing for it. (personal communication October 2015)

Therefore, traditional forms continue but under new conditions. I would argue that the 1930s photographs remind the viewer of an earlier type of life which still persists and that cannot be simply dismissed as embarrassing or indecorous.

The size of the Walkabout archive is a treasure to be preserved and studied further. The accounts of this adventure also provides us with a snapshot of exploration and the circumstances that made it possible. The preservation of the subsequent archive by both Guinness and Delves Broughton families now means that a well-resourced deposit is freely available in the Royal Anthropological Institute's visual records, as well as at the British Museum, Cambridge University Museum of Archaeology and Anthropology, the Pitt Rivers Museum, Oxford, and at the Asmat Museum of Culture and Progress in Agats, Asmat.

References

Anderson, Benedict, 1991: *Imagined Communities: Reflections on the Origin and Spread of Nationalism*, rev. edn, Verso, London.

Azoulay, Ariella, 2008: *The Civil Contract of Photography*, Zone Books, New York.

—, 2012: *Civil Imagination*, Verso, London.

Ballard, Chris, 2001: 'The visual exploration of New Guinea', in Chris Ballard, Steven Vink and Anton Ploeg, *Race to the Snow: Photography and the Exploration of Dutch New Guinea, 1907–1936*, Royal Tropical Institute, Amsterdam, pp. 7–9.

Beaglehole, J.C., 1955: *The Journals of Captain James Cook on his Voyages of Discovery. The Voyage of the* Endeavour *1768–1771*, Cambridge University Press, Cambridge.

Bell, Joshua A., Brown, Alison K. and Gordon, Robert J. 2013: *Recreating First Contact: Expeditions, Anthropology and Popular Culture*, Smithsonian Institution Press, Washington, D.C.

Bloemen, Fons, 1998: *First Contact: Original Reports of the Initial Encounters between Europeans and Papua's of South New Guinea from the Seventeenth until the Twentieth Century*, Jabeek, Netherlands.

Boelaars, Jan, 1981: *Head-hunters about Themselves: An Ethnographic Report from Irian Jaya, Indonesia*, Martinus Nijhof, The Hague.

Bond, Brian and Robbins, Simon 1987: *Staff Officer: The Diaries of Lord Moyne 1914–1918*, Leo Cooper, London.

Braunholtz, Herman Justus, 1934: 'Carved shields and spears from Dutch New Guinea', *The British Museum Quarterly*, vol. VIII (1933–4), pp. 153–5.

—, 1936: 'Note on a special exhibition of ethnographical objects from New Guinea and Indonesia collected by Lord Moyne, P.C., and D.S.O.', *Man* (June), pp. 95–6.

—, 1937: 'Ethnographical collection from New Guinea', *British Museum Quarterly*, vol. XI (1936–7), pp. 163–7.

British Museum, 1934: Accessions Register, items Oc.1934.0316.1-93.

—, 1936: Accessions Register, items Oc1936.0720.197-316.

Brodie, Marc, 2008: 'Guinness, Walter Edward, first Baron Moyne 1880–1944', *Oxford Dictionary of National Biography*, Oxford University Press, p. 214.

Carter, Paul, 1992: *Living in a New Country: History, Travelling and Language*, Faber and Faber, London.

—, 2004: *Material Thinking: The Theory and Practice of Creative Research*, Melbourne University Press, Carlton, Victoria.

Churchill, Clementine, 1935: letter to Winston Churchill from the estuary of the Eilanden River, Dutch New Guinea, 30 January, Churchill College Cambridge, The Sir Winston Churchill Archive Trust, CHAR 1/273/24.

Clarke, Louis, 1936a: letter to Captain Bill Spencer, 26 May, Cambridge University Museum of Archaeology and Anthropology archives.

—, 1936b: memo to staff, Cambridge University Library, A.C. Haddon Collection, Envelope 3035.

Connolly, Bob and Anderson, Robin, 1987: *First Contact: New Guinea's Highlanders Encounter the Outside World*, Viking Penguin, New York.

Corbey, Raymond, 2010: *Headhunters from the Swamp: the Marind Anim of New Guinea as seen by the Missionaries of the Sacred Heart, 1905–1925*, KITVL Press, Leiden.

Davenport Hines, Richard, 2004: 'Sir (Henry John) Delves [Jock] Broughton', *Oxford Dictionary of National Biography*, vol. 25, p. 1026.

Delves Broughton, Vera, 1935a: 'Komodo dragons at home: new specimens for the zoo', *The Times* (2 May), p. 18.

—, 1935b, 'Cruise of the *Rosaura*', *The Times* (23 May), p. 20.

Douglas, A.J.A. and Johnson, P.H. 1926: *The South Seas of Today: Being An Account of the Cruise of the Yacht St. George to the South Pacific*, Cassell and Co., London.

Helfrich, Klaus, 1996: 'The Asmat', in Gunter and Ursula Konrad (eds), *Asmat Myth and Ritual: The Inspiration of Art*, Erizzo Editrice, Venice, pp. 35–43.

Irwandi, Joshua, 2014: 'Not a blank canvas', unpublished MA thesis, London College of Communication, University of the Arts, London.

Miley, Brooke, 2008: 'Lord Moyne's collection at the University of Oxford's Pitt Rivers Museum of Anthropology and world archaeology: a brief note', Pitt Rivers Museum, Oxford.

Moore, Clive, 2003: *New Guinea: Crossing Boundaries and History*, University of Hawai'i Press, Honolulu.

Moyne, Lord (Walter Edward Guinness), 1934: letter to H.J. Braunholtz, 7 March, Centre for Anthropology Archives, British Museum, Eth Doc 1004.
—, 1935a: 'A Melanesian cruise: the voyage of the *Rosaura* among the head hunters', *The Times* (23 May), pp. 17–18.
—, 1935b: 'Islands of the Western Pacific', *Country Life* (29 June), pp. 673–6.
—, 1936a: *Walkabout: A Journey in Lands between the Pacific and Indian Oceans*, William Heinemann, London.
—, 1936b: 'Bush creatures of uncertain origins, friendly warriors, crudely garbed and armed', *Daily Telegraph* (5 June).
—, 1936c: letter to Dr A.C. Haddon, 21 June, Cambridge University Library Haddon Collection, envelope 3035.
—, 1936d: letter to Henry Balfour, 1 July, Pitt Rivers Museum manuscript collection, Balfour papers, Box 6 Item 12.
—, 1936e: letter to Louis Clarke, 29 May 1936, Cambridge University Museum of Archaeology and Anthropology correspondence files.
—, 1950: 'China: a young man's first encounter', *The Geographical Magazine* (June), pp. 41–8.
Netherland Committee for International Nature Protection, 1938: *Report Concerning the Possibility of Protecting the Primitive Natives, Especially the Mountain-Papuan-tribes in Dutch New Guinea*, Amsterdam, The Colonial Institute.
Newbury, Darren, 2015: 'Relocating the Heseltine photographic collection at District Six Museum', *African Arts* 48:2, pp. 64–77.
Nova Guinea, 1923: vol. VII, *Ethnographie*, 'Résultats des expeditions scientifiques néerlandaises à la Nouvelle Guinée en 1907, 1909, 1912, 1913 et 1920 sous les auspices de Dr H.A. Lorentz, A. Franssen Herderschee and A.J.A. van Overeem', E.J. Brill, Leiden.
Ohoiwirin, John, 2011: *Portret Pastor Geraldus Zegwaard, MSC, Bersama umat Asmat Kampung Syru Misi Perdana 1950-an*, Divisi Dokumentasi dan Penelitian, Museum Kebudayaan dan Kemajuan Asmat, Keuskupan Asmat, Agats.
Quanchi, Max, 2007: *Photographing Papua: Representation, Colonial Encounters and Imaging in the Public Domain*, Cambridge Scholars Publishing, Newcastle.
Rawlings, C.G., 1913: *The Land of the New Guinea Pygmy: An Account of the Story of a Pioneer Journey of Exploration into the Heart of New Guinea*, Seeley Service and Co., London.
Rockefeller, Michael Clark, 1967: *The Asmat of New Guinea: The Journal of M.C. Rockefeller, Museum of Primitive Art, New York.*
Saulnier, Tony, 1963: *Headhunters of Papua*, Paul Hamlyn, London.
Singapore Free Press and Mercantile Advertiser, 12 November 1935: 'Yachting cruise plans kept secret: Lord Moyne interviewed in Singapore', p. 10.
Sowada, Alphonse A., 2002: 'The decline, suppression and rejuvenation of Asmat culture and art: an historical approach', in Ursula Konrad, Alphonse Sowada and Gunter Konrad (eds), *Asmat Perception of Life in Art: The Collection of the Asmat Museum of Culture and Progress*, Mönchengladbach, B. KühlenVerlag, pp. 47–64.
Stanley, Nick, 2012: *The Making of Asmat Art: Indigenous Art in a World Perspective*, Sean Kingston Publishing, Canon Pyon.
—, forthcoming: 'Robert Goldwater and the search for the primitive: the Asmat project at the Museum of Primitive Art', in Pam Meecham (ed.), *Companion to Modern Art*, Wiley, Chichester.
Stasch, Rupert, 2011: 'Textual iconicity and the primitivist cosmos: chronotypes of desire in travel writing about Korowai of West Papua', *Journal of Linguistic Anthropology*, vol. 21, issue 1, pp. 1–21.
Suharto, 1969: 'Heart to heart talk by President Suharto at the gathering for the West Irian Humanitarian Project', in *President Suharto's Operation Humanity Project for the Development of West-Irian*, Bogor, 9 November, pp. 7–17.
Swadling, Pamela 1996: *Plumes from Paradise: Trade Cycles in Outer Southeast Asia and their Impact on New Guinea and Nearby Islands until 1920*, Papua New Guinea National Museum, Boroko.
Sydney Morning Herald, 7 February 1935.
van Duuren, David and Steven Vink, 2011: 'Expeditions: collecting and photographing', in D. van Duuren (ed.), *Oceania at the Tropenmuseum*, KIT Publishers, Amsterdam, pp. 47–99.
Villevoye, Roy, 2008: *Detours*, Museum van Boijmans Beuningen, Rotterdam.
Wollaston, Alexander Frederick Richmond, 1933: *Letters and Diaries of A.F. Wollaston*, selected and edited by Mary Wollaston, Cambridge University Press.
Zegwaard, Gerard MSC, 1952: 'In het land van de menseneters', *Annalen van Onze Lieve Vrouw van het Heilig Hart* 66 (10), pp. 136–8.
—, 1955: 'Asmat history: contact till 1955', in Frank A. Trenkenschuh OSC, *Asmat Sketch Book 2, Agats, Irian Jaya and Hastings, Nebr. Asmat Museum of Culture and Progress and Crosier Missions*: 5–24, 2nd edition. Translated by Frank A. Trenkenschuh OSC.

Index

Page numbers in *italic* refers to captions only

arrows 7, 28, 36, 38, 40
art 4, 13, 16, 39, 40, 44, 47
Asmat Foundation (YKPA) 48
Asmat Museum of Culture and Progress 40, 50, 51
Aura *8*, 11, *14*
Azoulay, Ariella 50

Balfour, Henry 12, 47
Bloemen River 3, 11, 12, 17, *19*–21, 39, 40, 47, *49*
birds of paradise and their feathers 6, 7, 17, 29, 35, 36, 38
bone/s
  daggers; *see* crocodile-jaw-bone daggers
  human 21, 47; *see also* skulls
  ornaments 5
  pig jaws 20
Boelaars, Jan 29
bottles 35, 36, 38
bowls *32*, 38, 40
Braunholtz, Herman Justus 4, 12, 17, 18, 20, 39, *40*, 45, 47
British Museum (BM) v, 1, 3, 4, 9, 10, 12, 13, 47, 48, 51
  Oc1934,0316 series v, *40*–*43*
  Oc1936,0720 series v, *10*, *41*, *42*, *43*
  Oc,B28 series v, *10*, *19*

Cambridge University Museum of Archaeology and Anthropology (until 1978 Cambridge University Museum of Archaeology and Ethnology) 4, 10, 48, 51
canoes 5–7, 16, 17, 21–6, 28, 29, 33–5, 43, 48, 50
Carter, Paul 29
Churchill, Clementine 9, 11–13, 28
Clarke, Louis 10, 47
clothing 12, 17, 46, 51; *see also* nakedness
contemporary Asmat 1, 40–*43*, 45, 48–51
Cook, James 5, 6
crocodile-jaw-bone daggers 10, 40, 43, *49*

daggers *see* crocodile-jaw-bone daggers
dance 28–30, 40, *43*
Delves Broughton, Rosamond 10, *21*, 35–8, 49
Delves Broughton, Vera v, 3–*5*, *8*–*11*, *13*, *14*, *19*–25, *27*–38, 48, 49
deserted villages 17–21, 47, 49, 50
Digul River 3, 6
Doyussi River 3, 7, 17
drums 20, 40, *42*, 45
Dutch colonial/military presence 3, 6, 7, 12–13, 15, 51

Eastern Cruise 1934/35 album v, *3*, *9*, *11*, *13*, *27*, *30*
Eastern Trip 1935–36 album v, 13, *21*, *23*, *24*, *28*, *32*, *33*, *35*, *36*
Eilanden River 3, 5, 7, *8*, 12–*15*, *18*, *19*, 21–*34*, 38–40, 47, 49
Elveden, Arthur v, 4, 9, 10, 13, 15, 18, *21*, *27*, 28–30, 34, 36, *38*, 45, 48–50
exchange 1, 6, 7, 10, 13, 16, 17, *23*, 25, *27*, 31–8, 49, 51; *see also* traders

friends, friendly relations 1, 5, 7, 13, 16, 28, 34, 38, 40, 47

Haddon, A.C. 12, 45
head-hunters 6, 7; *see also* skulls

history 1, 5, 14–16, 45, 48, 50, 51
horns 40, *42*, 45
house posts 18–*20*, 40, *41*, 48, 49

Indonesia 6, 16, 47, 48, 50, 51
Irwandi, Joshua 51

Jayawijaya Mountains 2, 3, 6, 12
je (men's house) 38, 40, *41*, 48

Kampong River 3, 7, *10*, 12–14, 17, 21–3, 28, 31, 34–9, 47, 49

Leahy, Michael 16
London Zoo 1, 10
'lovely girl' 13, 28–31, 50; *see also* women (Asmat)

Marind Anim 45
masks 20, 47, 51
mats 31, 34
men's house *see je*
Meyjes, J.P. and de Rochemont, E.J. 6, 36
missionaries 15, 39, 40, 45, 51
Missionaries of the Sacred Heart 15
modern Asmat *see* contemporary Asmat
Mount Wilhemina *see* Jayawijaya Mountains
Moyne, Lord (Walter Edward Guinness)
 biography 8–9
 first trip to Asmat (1929) 3, 7, 9, 13, 15, 16, 17, 28, 39, 45; *see also* Travels WEG album
 second trip to Asmat (1934–5) v, 3, 7, 9, 12–14, 25, 28, 47; *see also* British Museum Oc.1934,0316 series; Eastern Cruise 1934/35 album
 third trip to Asmat 3–4, 9, 10, 12–14, 28, 45, 47; *see also* British Museum Oc1936,0720 series; Eastern Trip 1935–36 album; Walkabout

nakedness 6, 12, 13, 51; *see also* clothing
necklaces 25, *28*, 35
Nova Guinea v, *6*, *7*, 12

Otakwa River 6, 12

paddles 7, 13, 21, 23, *34*, 36, 47, 48; *see also* spears
Pereira, Arthur v, 4, 10, *19*, 21, *22*, 25, *26*, 34, 48
performance 28–31; *see also* dance
Pitt Rivers Museum 4, 12, 47, 48, 51
poles
 ancestor (*bisj*) 43, 44
 ceremonial 18, 19; *see also* house posts

Quanchi, Max 14–16

Rawlings, Cecil Godfrey 6
Roche, Richard 7, 16, 17, 34, 38
Rockefeller, Michael 16, 43
Rosaura 10–12, 14, *15*, 18, 48
Rose 11
Roussalka, MY 9, 11
Royal Anthropological Institute (RAI) v, 4, 12–15, *22*, *29*, *37*, 47, 51
 RAI 400 series v, *5*, *8–11*, *13*, *14*, *19–21*, *24–6*, *31*, *32*, *37*
Royal College of Surgeons 51
Royal Colonial Institute (Amsterdam) 15, 47

shields 5, 7, 13, *15*, 17–19, 21, *22*, 39–40, 45, 47, 49
skulls 6, 10, 12, 13, 20–2, 48; *see also* bones, human
spears 7, 13, 21, 23, *34*, 36, 38, 40, 47; *see also* paddles
Stasch, Rupert 6
Swadling, Pamela 6

TM series v, *6*, *7*
traders 5, 7, 36–8, 40, 45; *see also* exchange; Roche, Richard
Transfer film footage v, 33
Travels WEG album v, *8*, *9*, *17*, *18*, *44*

Walkabout *see also* Moyne, third trip to Asmat
 archive 1, 4, 16, 51
 book *2–5*, *9–11*, 13–16, 21, *22*, *27*, *34*, *40*, *49*, *50*
 exhibition 1, 4, 14, 15, 45–7
 film v, 4, 17, *18*, *27–30*, *34*, 36, *38*, 49
Wollaston, A.F.R. 12
women (Asmat) 16, 28, 29; *see also* 'lovely girl'

Yayasan Kemajuan dan Pengembanan Asmat (YKPA) *see* Asmat Foundation